Children, Teachers and Learning Series

Series Editor: Cedric Cullingford

Children and Society

WITHDRAWN

Titles in the *Children, Teachers and Learning* series

Children and Society
Children's Attitudes to Politics and Power

Cedric Cullingford

CASSELL

Cassell

Villiers House	387 Park Avenue South
41/47 Strand	New York
London WC2N 5JE	NY 10016–8810

© Cedric Cullingford 1992

First published 1992

British Library Cataloguing-in-Publication Data
A catalogue record for this book is available from the British Library.

Library of Congress Cataloging-in-Publication Data
Cullingford, Cedric.
　　Children and society: children's attitudes to politics and power/Cedric Cullingford.
　　　　p.　cm. — (Children, teachers and learning series)
　　Includes bibliographical references and index.
　　ISBN 0-304-32418-3 — ISBN 0-304-32437-X (pbk.)
　　1. Children and politics.　2. Political socialization.
　　3. Children — Great Britain — Attitudes.　I. Title.　II. Series:
　　Children, teachers and learning.
　　HQ784.P5C85　1992
　　303.3′880544 — dc20　　　　　　　　　　　　　　　　　　91–39856
　　　　　　　　　　　　　　　　　　　　　　　　　　　　　　　CIP

ISBN 0-304-32418-3 (hardback)
　　　0-304-32437-X (paperback)

Typeset by Colset Private Limited, Singapore
Printed and bound in Great Britain by
Biddles Ltd, Guildford and King's Lynn

Contents

For Christine and Terry Shepherd

Foreword

The books in this series stem from the conviction that all those who are concerned with education should have a deep interest in the nature of children's learning. Teaching and policy decisions ultimately depend on an understanding of individual personalities accumulated through experience, observation and research. Too often in recent years decisions on the management of education have had little to do with the realities of children's lives, and too often the interest shown in the performance of teachers, or in the content of the curriculum, has not been balanced by an interest in how children respond to either. The books in this series are based on the conviction that children are not fundamentally different from adults, and that we understand ourselves better by our insight into the nature of children.

The books are designed to appeal to *all* those who are interested in education and take it as axiomatic that anyone concerned with human nature, culture or the future of civilization is interested in education; in the individual process of learning, as well as what can be done to help it. While each book draws on recent findings in research, and is aware of the latest developments in policy, each is written in a style that is clear, readable and free from the jargon that has undermined much scholarly writing, especially in such a relatively new field of study.

Although the audience to be addressed includes all those concerned with education, the most important section of the audience is made up of professional teachers, the teachers who continue to learn and grow and who need both support and stimulation. Teachers are very busy people, whose energies are taken up in coping with difficult circumstances. They deserve material that is stimulating, useful and free of jargon and is in tune with the practical realities of classrooms.

Each book is based on the principle that the study of education is a discipline in its own right. There was a time when the study of the principles of learning and the individual's response to his or her environment was a collection of parts of other disciplines — history, philosophy, linguistics, sociology and psychology. That time is assumed to be over and the books address those who are interested in the study of children and how they respond to their environment.

Each book is written both to enlighten the readers and to offer practical help to develop their understanding. They therefore not only contain accounts of what we understand about children, but also illuminate these accounts by a series of examples, based on observation of practice. These examples are designed not as a series of rigid steps to be followed, but to show the realities on which the insights are based.

Most people, even educational researchers, agree that research on children's learning has been most disappointing, even when it has not been completely missing. Apart from the general lack of a 'scholarly' educational tradition, the inadequacies of such study come about because of the fear of approaching such a complex area as children's inner lives. Instead of answering curiosity with observation, much educational research has attempted to reduce the problem to simplistic solutions, by isolating a particular hypothesis and trying to prove it, or by trying to focus on what is easy and 'empirical'. These books try to clarify the real complexities of the problem, and are willing to be speculative.

The real disappointment with educational research, however, is that it is very rarely read or used. The people most at home with children are often unaware that helpful insights can be offered to them. The study of children and the understanding that comes from self-knowledge are too important to be left to obscurity. In the broad sense real 'research' is carried out by all those engaged in the task of teaching or bringing up children.

All the books share a conviction that the inner worlds of children repay close attention, and that much subsequent behaviour and attitudes depend upon the early years. The books also share the conviction that children's natures are not markedly different from those of adults, even if they are more honest about themselves. The process of learning is reviewed as the individual's close and idiosyncratic involvement in events, rather than the passive reception of, and processing of, information.

Cedric Cullingford

Preface

This is a book not only about how people learn and think but about the curriculum. It reflects on the practice of what goes on in schools.

The debate about the National Curriculum has mostly been conducted in terms of traditional subjects, as if there were so many heads of departments carving up the timetable according to their prowess in fighting for 'their' corner. There has been comparatively little analysis of the purpose of the curriculum. The material in this book shows how much children learn that lies outside the formal curriculum, and shows how they develop attitudes and prejudices that the formal curriculum ignores.

The attitudes that children develop have an impact on the traditional curriculum, as well as on their subsequent careers. How they approach the concepts that underlie geography and history, language and technology depends on the way they have learned to formulate their response to what they observe. They depend on their experience and informal discussion in forming essential concepts. And yet these concepts only obliquely relate to the curriculum as delivered in schools. Their impact is subtle, and rarely made use of.

Discussion about the implications of the findings in this book has taken place with too many people to single out some of them. But I have also received practical help. Whilst the children and schools remain as anonymous as which parts of the country they come from, I am grateful in particular to Harry Judge and the Oxford University Department of Educational Studies, to Peter Madgewick and the Oxford Polytechnic Research Committee, and to Liz Heath. I am also grateful for the interest and encouragement of Naomi Roth, and, of course, Nichola.

CHAPTER 1
Introduction

Children are as much a part of society as adults. We may have created separate institutions for them and even tried to suggest that 'childhood' is almost a separate status or category.[1] But they live in the same context, observe the same things. They think, analyse and question. They hold views on politics, on the economy and on the environment. And yet their views are almost always ignored. Surveys of attitudes and polls of political opinions cover small samples of the adult population as if they could represent all others. But there are few explorations of the developing ideas of children in their analysis of the world they live in which will influence the future. Why?

It is easy for adults to forget how early their views were formed and how influenced by their earliest experiences they remain. It is far easier to imagine that political opinions are so responsive to immediate events that they have only recently been refined. And the tendency to assume that other people's opinions are less sensible than one's own has, it seems, an easy target in children, about whom one can feel immensely superior. To accuse others of holding naïve or absurd opinions in itself implies personal maturity. And yet it is well known among political and social commentators that adult opinions about their society and its politics are not often well formed:

> The problem for the democrat is that on many issues the people's wishes are obscure, inarticulate or even non-existent; on other issues the people will be divided, some for, some against; and in some cases a democratic government may believe profoundly that all or most of the people are mistaken.[2]

If children do not have sophisticated and well-informed opinions and a close analysis of society, they are not the only ones. And yet it is an unquestioned assumption that children do not have political opinions until they suddenly acquire them when they are able vote.

1

The absence from the curriculum of any formal study of society or the 'constitution' suggests that children do not need to hold political opinions. Indeed, any analysis of political questions is actually frowned upon in educational legislation on the grounds that children would merely acquire prejudices rather than understanding. This is unlikely to be a deliberate result of the profound secretiveness of governments.[3] It is more likely to be an outcome of the sense that children have other things to learn than taking their part in society, that education for citizenship is not part of the curriculum. One reason for the lack of interest in children's opinions is this pervasive, unreflecting feeling that children's opinions are not worth taking seriously. The same demarcations that adults make with each other, between 'I' and 'them' —

'*I* have an individual, intelligent opinion.'
'*You* have an interesting point, but are wrong.'
'*They* are stupid.'

— place children firmly with 'them'.

It is easy to be sentimental about children, to assume that they are naïve, uncritical and innocent, that they have no interest in the events of the day, that they have no knowledge and no opinions, and that they do not wish to know. It is as if children should still be seen and not heard. And yet children do have opinions. They are aware of what is on the news. They observe and analyse the workings of authority both in their daily experience and in what they see of society as a whole. The attitudes of those who will be politicians as well as voters, and who will influence as well as be part of the future, are formed early. Children develop views towards authority and towards formal relationships with others in society long before they are expected to express their views in political terms. And this, perhaps, is where part of the misunderstanding lies.

'Politics' is a term often misconstrued as party politics. Those who would wish children to be kept far away from political discussion really mean that they want children to be protected from the views of their political rivals. They might be influenced or even brainwashed by the Right or the Left, as if it were not possible to analyse without bias. So children are forced to find out for themselves, in their own way, how the world of politics works and how it fits into the daily experience of society. Politics for children does not consist only of parties. In the wider sense, it embraces all kinds of authorities, rules and laws carried out by people in well-defined roles. Any party politics only makes sense in the framework of a permanent constitution.

Children acquire an understanding of politics in the wider sense very early. They have to learn about working co-operatively, understanding other points of view and negotiating outcomes.[4] They need to understand justice and fairness and the application of rules. But they also observe the success and failure of social relationships in others. They observe their parents and other adults as well as their peer group. And the consequences of success and failure in social events are presented in all their extremes on the television. Society is seen in terms of organized or disorganized masses. One of the most important experiences of school is the development of social understanding, seeing how power works and on what it is based, and observing the tensions between the individual and the crowd. Schools are microcosms of society. They give an essential grounding in politics, not deliberately but inevitably.

The society they grow up in is closely observed by children. They understand the role that party politics plays. By the age of 7 they have acquired a political vocabulary and a concept of the role of the Prime Minister.[5] Aged 8 they use political phrases with accuracy. But they have understood the rudiments of society much earlier. Long before children show an interest in the peculiar distinctions of policy they have acquired a grounding in power and control. Most of the literature on children and politics has explored what children *know*. This book, concerned with children and society, is about what children *think*. Their opinions are far more revealing than party allegiances.

Children's views of their society are revealing. They are also interesting. Many an assumption about what is (or isn't) in their minds is overturned by the consistency of their analysis. Whilst they might not use elaborate terms, or extensive analogies, the bases for future social action and political attitudes have already been laid. Children are not mere passive recipients of school rules, but active participants in their success or failure. They do not just imbibe the news but react to it. They hear political opinions constantly. They witness the hatreds expressed by political figures every day. They see the personalities behind the decisions. And they observe the individuals caught up in large-scale social events. All these matters force them into extending their opinions, not just trying to make coherent sense of what they see but finding means of expressing how they learn to react. Thus children develop their world view.

The lack of interest and attention paid to what children think has given rise to a number of assumptions. One is that education as a form of social control leads children to develop benevolent attitudes towards authority and institutions.[6] That children need to develop coherent attitudes is clear, but it does not follow that they view what they see with such optimism that they assume its moral rightness. When children observe how schools work they maintain the distance of critical analysis at the same time as being caught up in their own daily experiences. The kinds of attitudes developed are strong, but not always benevolent in the way that some critics would suggest.[7] The hegemony of a society does not imply that children are unaware of the anomalies within it. They understand contradictions as well as anybody.

The myth that children simply imbibe the values of the culture given to them needs exploration as well as questioning. It is, of course, easy to see the development of society as a matter of transferring sets of values from one generation to the next. But when this assumption is examined historically we see that there are many collective changes of consciousness that people undergo. Certain attitudes do not remain static, not even the attitude that cultural stereotypes are taken on board by children from their experience of schools. Schools, after all, vary in their sense of values: they vary in attitudes, towards styles of teaching and learning and towards discipline and organization. Schools are not stereotypes of authority. Even in their similarities, they are not taken, by children, at face value.

If one stereotype of children learning about society is the acceptance of half-hidden assumptions by the school, another is that children idealize not only institutions but political figures. Much has been made of public figures as political symbols, 'focal points to whom loyalty can be directed'.[8] The belief is that a generally benign feeling spreads from personal symbols to institutions, and vice versa. Thus children are supposed to view the ethos of the school they are in as one which can be transferred to politics as a whole, symbolized in benevolent public figures. The argument is whether such attitudes derive more from the influence of the family or the school,[9] as if it were possible to take for granted that children have no equivocal feelings about politicians and the State. It is as if a Piagetian rule of thumb had been applied to children's thinking patterns.[10] On both sides of the Atlantic observers conclude that children look on political figures and policemen with unmitigated awe, before they begin to develop a sense of the conflict of politics.[11] But, as we will see when we pursue children's interests in society, children have no such sense of an 'ideal norm'. Whilst children understand the role of the person in political life,[12] it does not follow that such a person is idealized.

Society is made up of individuals. From our own point of view this is obvious, despite the tendency to think of the rest of 'them' as an anonymous mass. But children also see individuals in action in society. They observe the talking head on television, the passionate politician, and the identikits of criminals. The question is how such forms of individuality fit into larger patterns, such as when crowds are observed working together, or in the massed ranks of the police, or on football terraces. Children understand the difference between individual and mass behaviour, between people reacting against institutions and those playing their parts within institutions. They also understand the hierarchies of society and the different status afforded to different people according to their job and their wealth. They know about class distinctions and connect such differences with politics.[13] It is because of this awareness of different aspects of power that children analyse the effectiveness and ineffectiveness of influence. Institutions are clearly made up of people who wield power. Influence arises from the closeness to the centres of power; and this depends on class. Children, therefore, develop a cool appraisal of institutions. The lack of a high level of pride in them connects with the low level of detailed interest in politics. Politics, class and influence are seen to work closely together.[14]

The focus of attention on schools as the most important sources of influence has itself led to assumptions about children's development of political interests. But once children's attitudes to society are explored, a different picture emerges. There are many other influences brought to bear, and schools are then seen in a wider context. Whether children see schools as benign or not, they do not simply transfer their observation of schools to society. They observe everyday politics in action, certainly, at home and on television. What they observe in school has a context, and reveals examples of failure as well as success, of unfairness and arbitrariness as well as benevolence. Schools might *prepare* children in their development of attitudes more strongly than they inculcate facts, but children also *anticipate* their later political and social views through the association of many pieces of information.[15]

If education is seen as a form of social control then it is important to gather evidence from those ostensibly controlled. It emerges that children's attitudes towards society are not as naïve as might be supposed, nor as simply optimistic. If there is a 'covert mobilization of bias',[16] then one should begin to wonder whether the outcomes that children reveal are really the norms that society wishes to pass on. Children do not see society in exactly the same terms as a school, for they observe organized conflict, political bias, and the whole structure of social services and the reasons for their existence. They are witnesses to the realities of society from an early age. But they also observe the realities of school, with outside pressures brought to bear on the headteacher, and the amount of negotiations and discussion that surrounds decisions. Politics, in terms of laws and the people who make them, are what makes society. Children understand politics in those terms long before they articulate their attitudes in party political terms.

NOTES AND REFERENCES

1. Elias, N. *The Civilising Process*: Vol. 1, *The History of Manners*. 1978; Vol. 2, *State Formation and Civilisation*. 1982. Oxford: Blackwell.

2. Madgewick, P. *Introduction to British Politics*. London: Hutchinson, 1976, p. 17.

3. Madgewick, P., *op. cit.*, p. 304.

4. Dunn, J. *The Beginnings of Social Understanding*. Oxford: Blackwell, 1988.

5. Stevens, O. *Children Talking Politics: Political Learning in Childhood*. Oxford: Martin Robertson, 1982.

6. Whitmarsh, G. 'The politics of political education. An episode.' *Journal of Curriculum Studies* 6(1), 133–142, 1974.

7. Gramsci, A. *Selections from Prison Notebooks*. London: Lawrence and Wishart, 1978.
   Bowles, S., and Gintis, H. *Schooling in Capitalist America*. London: Routledge and Kegan Paul, 1976.

8. Stradling, R., and Zurick, E. 'Political and non-political ideals of English primary and secondary school children.' *Sociological Review* **19**(2), 203–227, 1971.
9. Hyman, H. *Political Socialization*. New York: Free Press of Glencoe, 1959. Hess, R., and Torney, J. *The Development of Political Attitudes in Children*. Chicago: Aldine Press, 1967.
10. Stevens, J., *op. cit.*
11. Hess, R., and Torney, J., *op. cit.*
12. Greenstein, F. *Children and Politics*. New Haven: Yale University Press, 1965.
13. Dowse, R., and Hughes, J. 'The family, the school and the political socialization process.' *Sociology* **5**(1), 21–45, 1971.
14. Abrahamson, P. 'The differential political socialization of English secondary school students.' *Sociology of Education* **40**(3), 246–269, 1967.
15. Hess, R., and Torney, J., *op. cit.*
16. Whitmarsh, G., *op. cit.*, p. 133.

CHAPTER 2

The Individual Experience

'Well, I was watching the news yesterday and they said that a lady had been punched by a policeman and I think sometimes they go a bit far by handling the people when they're rioting. But they have to be quite rough, otherwise they're not going to get anywhere.' *(girl, 10)*

Talking is one of the favourite activities of human beings. The desire to communicate, to share a story, to relate an anecdote or an opinion is an important part of experience. It is so important that it sometimes prevents people listening. We only have to overhear conversations in a bus, or a bar or in a classroom to note how everyone becomes impatient for their own turn to speak. It is one's *own* experience of the dentist or the holiday that is the burning issue. Talking helps to define what people think. It makes experience real.

Talk is also the most powerful evidence of what people think and feel. Each wants to express opinions and relate how they have arrived at them. The only way to understand what is going on in people's minds is to hear what they say. And yet talk, as evidence, tends to be underrated. It is rare for evidence to be gathered from the most powerful source. This is because talking has a bad reputation. It is associated, more often than not, with the spread of rumour or gossip. The power of anecdote which informs political judgement more certainly than any 'evidence' is both used and feared. Hearing about an actual experience makes more impression that any statistic. So when researchers think of talk they think of single stories that sway political opinions against the weight of statistical evidence. They see all the dangers of believing anecdotes whilst knowing that their own are true.

The spoken or written word is the one source of understanding what people think. Given the opportunity to expand and define, it is the only way fully to comprehend what is going on in the mind. It is therefore the true basis of scientific evidence, far more so than questionnaires. Opinion polls often ask interviewees for answers of 'yes' or 'no' to complex questions.[1] However statistically satisfying it is to work out a factor analysis on the responses, the original material would have been more true if the subject could define what he or she was saying: 'yes; but . . .' The real difficulty, then, with trying to find out what people think is not the suspicion that the answer might be disagreeable, or wrong, but the time it takes to record, transcribe and analyse the information. The spoken word, which defines as best it can attitudes and opinions that are as complex as true, is the most important, and least used, means of gathering information.

Psychiatrists have long known this. In order to reach inside people's minds they have learned to listen, to let their subjects explore and reveal what they discover. Psychiatrists use language to discover far more hidden matters than opinions about others. They see language as able, through symbolic interaction and associations, to reveal inmost thoughts. If speaking can produce that, it can also reveal attitudes to less personal things. The spoken word, as well as the word in literature, reveals what simple tests leave unexplored.

Anthropologists have also long known this. Their attempts to understand other cultures have been based on the significance of carefully gathered scientific evidence, objectively assessed. They have not tried to test pre-judged hypotheses. Nor have they based any assumptions about sex or class or race on what they wished to discover. The scientific integrity of the anthropologist depends on the willingness to listen, to absorb information disinterestedly and objectively. And yet, despite, or perhaps because of, a lengthy anthropological tradition, such evidence has rarely been sought from cultures closer to home, and even more rarely from children. Fortunately, the realization has dawned that ethnography has an important part to play, together with the realization that it brings forward important empirical findings.[2] As yet, ethnographic techniques might have been more developed with adults, but children also need to be heard and understood.

The evidence that language gives is not just anecdotal. When children explore their ideas they reveal underlying attitudes and considered judgements, supported by emotions and instincts. In this way they make good subjects. Rather than pretend to have an opinion when they haven't one they will easily say, 'don't know'.

They prefer not to think rather than to invent an answer. They will venture to explore their ideas rather than follow a party line or try to please the interviewer. Naturally, part of the technique of gathering evidence is not to suggest that there are any right answers, or particular expectations. But children prove to be naturally fluent. They find it easy to hold opinions and to express them. In the course of a school day the teacher will often be told a series of personal intimacies and opinions. When enough of these opinions are gathered we find both the truthful idiosyncrasies of the individual and a lot of common ground. The true picture of what children think then emerges.

Despite the importance of language, there is still a certain amount of suspicion about what children say. This is partly because it is possible for children who are disturbed to fantasize, to create stories out of anecdotes and to begin not to know the difference between truth and fantasy. This is a sign of disturbance and relates clearly to fantasies rather than opinions. It is also an adult characteristic of those who are capable of inventing a story, say against a doctor, and telling lies in court. But this, too, is rare. For everyday needs it is difficult to avoid telling the truth. There is no purpose in lying. Children like to talk about what they think. They spend hours sharing opinions with each other. They have to form opinions. It is a rare opportunity for them, as well as adults, to find a ready listener.

The children in this research come from a variety of backgrounds. Whilst each of them has individual opinions and experiences and talks from a personal point of view, there is a remarkable unity amongst their individual opinions. The findings emerge from a number of individuals. It is the underlying agreements that are of greatest scientific interest, but one should not forget the scope for idiosyncrasy within the whole. The quotations give typical examples of what children say, but also have the authenticity of individuality. All the children of whatever age or background found it easy to talk and to explain, to think and explore for answers. But then they were not troubled with trying to find an answer. What they said emerged promptly and unselfconsciously.

The children were all interviewed individually. They came from a variety of primary schools 'somewhere in England'. The variety of schools included rural as well as urban ones, private schools as well as State-controlled. The sample of children was a random one, but included children from different ethnic and social backgrounds. No assumption was made about gender or class differences, and nothing emerged to suggest that they were significant or were underlying causes for any distinctions that could be imagined. The recording of age and sex with the quotations gives a sense of the individuality of each child; but the study does not emerge with significant developmental changes. By the age of 8 the underlying pattern seems to be set.

In the main bulk of the research, 215 children were interviewed. They came from 17 different schools. There were 97 boys and 118 girls, the slight imbalance reflecting the nature of the classes they came from. The interviews were with 23 7-year-olds, 43 8-year-olds, 65 9-year-olds, 49 10-year-olds and 35 11-year-olds. The quotations which illustrate the findings try to take a variety of samples from different ages and sexes, but the facts that emerge are consistent amongst all the children. The evidence presented is not a series of anecdotes but an overall picture of a frame of mind shared by the children. Their experiences have been formed neither in a large city nor in a place of particular urban blight. They come from a part of the country that has some unemployment (as they reveal) but has not been affected as badly as some areas of erstwhile heavy industry. Their experience includes the country, and villages, as well as towns.

In addition to the bulk of the research, a further survey of 150 children was carried out, mostly covering the material in Chapters 9 and 10, and including some 7- and 12-year-olds. These interviews were far shorter. The main research was dependent on interviews that lasted an hour. All the interviews were semi-structured; that is to say that there were certain things asked but the order in which they were asked would depend on how the children answered. The art of the interview was to suggest a conversation, a dialogue, even if the children did most of the talking. The interviewer had to be a good listener, put the child at his or her ease and give the individual the sense that whatever was said was interesting. Thus no one interview can be taken as typical of the rest. What is typical is the consistency of the answers.

The interviews took roughly the following form. The first few minutes were a general conversation, including information about

age, designed to accustom the children to the interviewer and overcome any self-consciousness, or consciousness of the tape recorder.
They were asked what subjects they liked, or about hobbies. All the
following questions were asked in as open a way as possible, without hinting that there were any correct answers. It was made clear
that the interviewer was interested in what they thought and was
not attempting to test their knowledge. The terms used were kept as
simple as possible; even words like 'politician' were avoided, so
when children volunteered information about politics it revealed
the extent of their awareness. After the opening conversation the
following questions were asked, not in the same words, not always
in the same order.

- who makes the rules in school?
- with help from anyone else?
- who makes the rules in Britain?
- with any help from others?
- how are the rules kept?
- how do the laws work?
- are all laws good ones?
- can one change the law?
- suppose you do not agree with the law?
- what happens if you don't?
- what do the police do?
- do you watch the news?
- do you talk about it?
- are things getting better or worse?

It was out of these open questions that various subjects were further
explored. Discussion about the police would lead to the children's
concern with football hooligans and rioters. These subjects were
not imposed on them. Sometimes the opening conversation would
include questions like, 'what do you do when you get home?' which
children would turn into a discussion of television viewing habits.
Out of the bland question of the 'rules' would emerge their strong
feelings about the law. Out of the general question of whether the
'person who makes the rules' — the Prime Minister, almost
inevitably — receives any support would emerge their picture of
the constitution, including Members of Parliament and the
Cabinet. With all the children all the major subjects were covered,

even if the order of the questions changed. Whilst the structure of the questions has been reduced to a checklist of about fifteen, the interviewer would ask many supporting questions, typically forty altogether.

All the interviews were then transcribed. Some of what the children said is rooted specifically in their own environment and in the time at which the interviews took place. The extracts taken from the children have avoided giving details which are specific to the time or place (for example, what was on the news at that time), because, at any one moment, even yesterday is dated. The form of the interview became established only after a pilot study that showed how the children revealed the kind of things they wished to talk about. The most important part of the evidence is the extraction of information from the transcriptions. When they were being read it was clear that certain themes emerged. These have become the themes of the book. They are not the same as the theme of the interview. What has emerged from the interviews was not dependent on any pre-judged hypothesis. Instead, it became clear that children consistently brought up major concerns, about law and order, about the police, and about the state of the world. This consistency is itself illuminating but can cause problems in tone. Consistency is not broad generalization. On careful analysis of all the transcripts it was obvious that whilst children differed somewhat in their knowledge of the constitution, and on their attitudes to the future, there were essential attitudes on which they all agreed. The quotations show the variety of ways in which they expressed their attitudes; but they all showed them. This does not lend itself to statistical sophistication, but it does underlie the essential truths.

There were no assumptions made at the start of the survey, beyond a curiosity about what children thought, and surprise at how little they had been asked. The initial interest lay in the children's ideas of politics, which is the one field in which researchers have shown some interest. Avoiding even the word 'politics' led the children into their attitudes towards society as a whole: politics in the broad sense of structures and constitutions, and the place of the individual in society. Thus the findings which emerge do so with the freshness of surprise rather than the palour of expectation. The data that the children present are clear and consistent. And they have implications that need exploring.

NOTES AND REFERENCES

1. Or 'Likert' scales, where the recipient of a questionnaire is asked to mark a five-point scale from 'strongly for' to 'strongly against'.
2. For example, the work of D. Hargreaves, M. Hammersley, P. Woods, A. Pollard and others.

CHAPTER 3

As Seen on Television: The Sources of Children's Information

'Sometimes I watch with Mum and Dad . . . We don't talk about it.'
(girl, 9)

By the time children are entitled to vote, they are assumed to have acquired enough political literacy to make significant decisions. These choices in voting are not just between political parties, but are concerned with what they stand for. A vote is a reflection of an attitude to the world, an opinion about the environment and the way it is developing, and an analysis of society. A vote reflects upbringing as well as judgement, and although it might be the outcome of unreasoned prejudice, it is also the result of weighing up and sifting a mass of complex evidence. How, then, do 18-year-olds acquire all the information on which an intelligent vote must be made?

There are, essentially, three possible sources, apart from personal observation: formal education, conversations with parents and peers, and the experience of the mass media. Whilst the experience of each child will be unique, virtually all will have had a mixture of all three sources, and will have developed attitudes that are a selection of other people's opinions and their own. But these attitudes will rarely have been formed through earnest study and discussion. The first political vote is as likely to be the result of a prejudice or fashion as well-considered beliefs. Whilst all children can be guaranteed to have experienced views of society conveyed by the media and to have formed opinions in conversation with others, not all children will have had much formal education about the society in which they live. Although social questions are addressed obliquely in the school curriculum they are rarely a central focus, either at the time when children first acquire social knowledge, or, years later, at the time they are entitled to vote.

The National Curriculum is traditional in its subject matter and has virtually no place for political education or sociology. It can be

15

argued, of course, that every subject can have social or political implications. History is a way of forming an understanding of how people live, and certainly the problems of geography are never far removed from political issues. But an analysis of society is not the central purpose in either discipline. Indeed, there is a marked suspicion of anything that could smack of political opinion-forming. This is for two reasons. The first affects older children. There is a fear that an analysis of issues, such as peace studies or economic awareness, could lead to indoctrination. Despite efforts like those of the Curriculum Review Unit or political literacy programmes, schools rarely tackle major issues, which might at most be dealt with under 'Current Affairs'. The school concentrates on a core curriculum, with its emphasis on skills and knowledge, leaving university students to grapple with controversy. It is as if children are not deemed ready to make sophisticated political or social judgements.

The second reason for the avoidance of controversy affects younger children. It is the argument that young children are incapable of forming sophisticated opinions, and unable to analyse political issues. Again, the idea of children as a *tabula rasa* on which other people's prejudices could be pressed leads to a contradiction. That children of 8 are able to discuss issues about the environment is clear. And yet the assumption that the curriculum should be free of all controversial issues means that children acquire their knowledge anywhere but in school. On the one hand, we expect children to have developed enough social literacy to make political judgements by the age of 18. On the other hand, we avoid giving them the means of acquiring such knowledge and analytical skills. In many schools there are opportunities for debates about issues such as hunting, zoos or pollution. But there are few occasions on which an analysis of the facts behind the issues, or what could be done about them, is central to the curriculum.

When children leave school they ponder about the relevance of a curriculum which is driven by the accumulation of fact rather than the analysis of these facts. When children are still in school the purpose of the curriculum is rarely addressed and they therefore fill this hiatus with their own interpretations of what school is for.[1] They see schools as preparing them for their futures, especially for jobs. And yet jobs, or the nature of the society in which they are placed, are rarely mentioned in school. The result of all this is that children acquire most of the information about the world they live in from informal sources: from their parents and peers, and the media.

Perhaps we take it for granted that children will reflect their parents' opinions and attitudes. Perhaps we feel it right and proper that schools should take no part in the development of people's opinions. But it is certainly during the school years that children acquire their fundamental attitudes, even if these attitudes remain half-formed prejudices rather than carefully weighed judgements. In these circumstances children develop their opinions in an oblique way, by overhearing comments and receiving anonymous advice. It has been argued that all opinions are formed in this way. Rather than responding to reasoned arguments, people tend to be more influenced by those they overhear.[2] And opinions, as Katz and Lazarsfeld demonstrated, are disseminated through other people, like 'gatekeepers',[3] so that individual attitudes are also social in character. There is a network of social interaction that forms rumours,[4] and the influence of gossip on opinions is well founded.[5] Conversations with peer groups are, therefore, a profoundly important part of developing opinions, even if (like all effects) they are difficult to pin-point.

Other people are, however, only one side of what is a triangle.[6] The individual is joined not only by parents or friends, but by the social collective messages of the mass media. Opinions of the world are formed by conversation and by observation; and by far the largest offerings to the latter are given by television.[7] To this extent television is a significant educational medium. It makes up for what the formal curriculum lacks. But the way in which television is received is itself very important, since children and their parents rarely analyse what they see. To understand what children know about society we need to understand how they learn what they know.

Children show little ostensible interest in politics, and yet they cannot avoid learning about it. The kind of interest they demonstrate naturally depends on how much conversation they have, especially with their parents. Only when there is an audience do we know their opinion; but it is also true that the earliest development of political points of view, let alone awareness, depends on the

17

amount of conversation with parents. If we take a survey of children, as a whole, whatever their parents' expressed interest in politics or their parents' willingness to discuss, over 80 per cent of children from the age of 8 state a preference for a particular political party.[8] This confirms that children have enough awareness of what is presented to them not only to understand the nature of politics but also to be able to make choices. Fear of party political propaganda has led to a suspicion of all mention of politics in school, even when politics are defined in the original meaning of the word, which includes all aspects of collective social life. The irony is that the increasing politicization of education is accompanied by fear of children discussing politics.

Children imbibe views presented to them on television, and reacted to by their parents. They might have little ostensible interest in politics, but then many of their parents do not have much interest either. The amount of interest children evince relates to the amount that their parents talk to them. Working-class children tend to talk much less with their parents.[9] But whatever the expressed interest, children are confronted with evidence of political activity almost every time they watch television, hear the radio, or read a newspaper. They also share views with each other, especially about events that make a major impact, or a long-running story, like the Falklands War. But as we will see, through the children's evidence, it is television that has the major impact, both because it is watched so much and because of the nature of its imagery. Other sources, like newspapers, can be easily ignored,

'I don't read newspapers . . .'

or read for other things than the news,

'News, boring, but newspapers . . . no, especially page three, not page three. There's really exciting things. On today's one there was *East-Enders* stuff and that lot.' *(boy, 8)*

On rare occasions newspapers are used in the classrooms.

'Well, we were doing a bit about it in our class. And we brought newspaper cuttings.' *(girl, 9)*

There is no news without politics, although some associate 'politics' with analysis or discussion of issues. The 'news' appears and reappears on television in a way that no children can completely avoid.

The daily ritual of children is well established. The return to home and tea after school is a re-entry, not just into a living room and family, but into a reminder of the outside world. The television is invariably on, even if in the background. Children watch a lot of television. The average amount of time is something in the region of three hours per day, although such a figure includes different styles of viewing and does not imply that children remain absorbed in all they see for that length of time. It is also well established that children prefer those programmes that are least demanding. Like an adult audience, they view television as a source of entertainment and avoid documentaries. They prefer soap operas and thrillers to children's programmes. They do not show any great pleasure in watching the news, since it is not always entertaining and contains a disproportionate amount of talking in relation to action. Many children would avoid watching the news if they were able to watch any other programme.

Nevertheless, whether they prefer to or not, children actually do watch the news on television almost every evening. The television scheduling, from the time that they get home to the bulk of the favourite evening programmes, includes news on all channels. Since the television is left on, or is switched on when the children come home, the news is overheard, or noticed, or even ostensibly ignored. The children in these interviews again confirm viewing habits discovered in earlier surveys, particularly their readiness to watch television whilst remaining apparently indifferent to it. When we discover how much they know about aspects of the news, it is clear that children have, in one way or another, learned a great deal about the issues. When we hear them talk about some of their attitudes to the police, or football hooligans, it is clear that many of the images they cite have been presented on television. Television, therefore, as the major presenter of current affairs, and as an essential focus of attention in the home, is a central source of information. There are a few children who see newspapers, and some who talk about events in the classroom with the teacher or their friends, but these are a small minority compared to those who every evening sit in front of the television by themselves or with their parents.

Children watch television as a matter of routine, every night.

There might be occasions when they also play with their friends, or go to another activity, but even then the television plays some part in their evening.

> 'I watch quite a lot. Mum doesn't like me watching it though.' *(girl, 10)*

> 'Usually I go to the biscuit tin and get a biscuit, and I get the little kitten and put it on my bed and watch television . . . sometimes it can be boring but sometimes it can be interesting.' *(boy, 10)*

The children were all asked what they did when they got home from school. The fact that all mentioned television shows how pervasive it is. They were quite critical of some aspects of what they had seen, and had clear preferences. But having clear preferences did not prevent them viewing other programmes without particular pleasure.

> 'I mostly stay in and watch telly.' *(girl, 10)*

> 'Mess about, watch with my parents.' *(boy, 10)*

> 'Well, I normally just sit and watch TV because I haven't got many friends around where I live.' *(boy, 9)*

Many children come home and find the television is already on. Watching is a natural part of the evening ritual, to be fitted in with other activities.

> 'I take my coat off and go and watch television.' *(girl, 7)*

> 'Well I usually sit down and watch some television. I watch John Craven's *Newsround* and then sometimes I watch a bit of the *Six O'Clock News*.' *(girl, 9)*

> 'Well, I watch telly until six o'clock and then I do my homework.' *(girl, 10)*

> 'Go in, put the telly on . . . children's ITV and then turn over to BBC 1.' *(girl, 10)*

> 'Well, I normally watch TV when I come home. It's normally on when I get home because my Dad watches it.' *(boy, 10)*

> 'Take my coat off. Go in the living room. See the cat. Go and watch the telly; anything that's on really.' *(boy, 10)*

The fact that television is left switched on has several consequences. It means that some of the time it is ignored, or only half-heartedly attended to, and looked at intermittently, with attention paid particularly to the most spectacular items. Other routines or necessities like homework or tea are also built round the television schedules, so that television acts as a kind of reprieve.

'Well, I go and watch telly but then it's tea so I have to have tea and then after tea I go and watch telly again.' *(girl, 8)*

'I usually watch it while I'm having my tea at six o'clock.' *(boy, 11)*

'Usually go upstairs and see what's on television. Then come down and have something to eat.' *(girl, 11)*

'I take my coat off and hang it up and take my lunch box out of my bag and give it to Mum and sit down and have a drink and TV.' *(girl, 10)*

Watching the television is as much a part of the usual routine of being home in the evening as having tea. When there is homework children tend to fit it around the television schedules or do it at the same time as watching.

'I have to go straight to my bedroom and do my homework . . . then watch TV.' *(girl, 9)*

'First I do my homework, and then my guitar practice, and then I usually clean out my hamster's cage . . . I watch TV by myself.' *(boy, 11)*

'Well, I sometimes watch the news but it's near my dinner time so I have to get on with my homework and then do my French project.' *(boy, 8)*

'If I have any homework, I get on with my homework . . . And watch telly.' *(girl, 11)*

Whatever other tasks that children carry out during the evening — seeing their friends, playing the guitar or reading comics (one child mentions reading a book) — the television is invariably mentioned as part of the arrangements. Most children are not very precise about what they watch, partly because they watch so much and partly because the act of viewing is more important than what is viewed. None the less this habit of indifferent viewing takes place in the context of clearly held preferences, and a knowledge of the schedules.

'Well, I usually go upstairs and I take off my coat and put it in the wardrobe, then I come down and watch *Young Doctors*.' *(girl, 9)*

21

'Mostly I get upstairs, get dressed and watch TV: *The Jet Set*. It's on Tuesday, Wednesday and Thursdays.' *(boy, 9)*

Watching television is both a private and a collective experience. Each viewer has his or her own perspective on television, and reaction to it. And yet members of a family tend to gather around a shared television, making occasional conversation and some comments about what they see. The television gives them the ease of being silent with each other, but is a common ground for their opinions. They might disagree about which programme to watch, but these disagreements do not seem very significant since most viewers accept that much of what they watch will not be of intense interest. Only rarely is there a suggestion of discriminating choice:

'Then I either watch television . . . it depends what's on. I have a look in the paper and see if there's any programmes that I like and then I just watch them.' *(girl, 11)*

Usually, whatever is on, even if not a favourite, is accepted.

The news is almost invariably part of an early evening's viewing. Children would not usually choose to watch the news, but see it as an unavoidable part of scheduling — 'If it comes on I have to watch it.' There is little evidence of great enthusiasm, but a lot of evidence that the news programmes are not only submitted to, but remembered. There are programmes like John Craven's *Newsround* as well as the *Six O'Clock News*, all referred to specifically by children. Even if they do not want to see them, their parents do; even if there is a general lack of interest, the news still appears.

'I do watch the news. Well, my mother usually watches it but otherwise I watch it by myself.' *(girl, 9)*

Even if they can avoid it, many children will submit to the news rather than turning off the television or leaving the room and doing something else. They are not forced to watch it by their parents, for there is little dialogue about what they see, but watch what they do not particularly wish to see.

'Go and sit down and watch television . . . But I think the telly's quite boring when the news comes on.' *(girl, 11)*

'I watched the news one night because it was before *Crossroads* and I watched that with Mummy.' *(girl, 8)*

'News is unavoidable in my Mum's case.' *(boy, 10)*

'I play on my computer, watch TV . . . news is a bit boring at times.' *(boy, 9)*

The children accept watching the news because their parents watch it. Sitting in front of the television is clearly a central experience for the family, not talking about what they see, but observing it, and perhaps making comments. Even if there are a number of programmes that children watch by themselves, there are others, like the news in particular, where the experience of watching is usually shared.

'I watch television . . . I watch it by myself . . . and my Mum and Dad sometimes.' *(girl, 8)*

'I watch it with Mummy because Daddy's still at work.' *(boy, 11)*

The sharing of television is not a deliberate matter, a desire of the family to come together to enjoy a particular programme, or discuss the ideas that television presents. It is simply a consequence that follows from the fact that the television is on, and because the family congregates for part of the time in the living room.

'Have something to eat sometimes. Watch TV news, sometimes if there's anything good on it. Parents usually know about it. Some of it's boring but some of it's quite good.' *(boy, 10)*

'Go in, put the telly on . . . news sometimes, it's sort of boring to me but interesting to them, and sometimes it's interesting.' *(girl, 10)*

'Well, I watch *Coast to Coast* with my parents and I sometimes see the headlines on the *Six O'Clock News.*' *(girl, 9)*

'Other times I just watch television. It depends who's in the room. Normally my parents.' *(boy, 10)*

The watching of television news is a mixture of ritual and the casual. Some items will hold more interest than others, but that is a matter of presentation rather than the inherent significance of the subject. Whilst children accept that their parents might wish to pay attention to certain news items, children do not generally follow particular stories with interest, unless there is a long-running story which they can, to some extent, anticipate. The news is seen as a series of stories, some shocking and some revealing. These stories present a series of pictures of the world: of wars and scandals, of rapes and murders, of a series of highlights and confrontations on which journalists depend. The impact of the news can therefore be at a variety of levels. Some stories will demand and receive close attention from children. Others will be a matter of complete indifference. Some stories linger in children's minds, despite their seeming lack of interest. Many stories make a cumulative impact, creating a series of pictures which reveal a general trend, like violence against the police or complaints against the law. But few of these items of news appear to be discussed at any length.

Children watch the news because it is on television and they know quite a number of details that are a matter of debate. But the details tend to be noted casually. Children watch with their parents; indeed, they watch the news because their parents watch it. But this does not mean that many children talk about what they see. It is as if they accepted that what is presented will obviously evoke particular attitudes, as if they took it for granted that the issues are understood.

Watching television is, perhaps, the most time-consuming activity which a family shares. When television carries news bulletins it transmits matters of universal importance as well as matters of direct relevance to the parochial lives of the audience. The relationship between two viewers and what is seen on the screen can reveal attitudes of control or *laissez-faire*.[10] They can make a great deal of difference to the development of ideas and perspectives in children. But those subjects which elicit dialogue, rather than expletives, are rare.

'Talk to parents, sometimes, about what does something mean or something like that . . . what does rape mean or something like that . . . well, there was this girl, she got raped . . .' *(girl, 10)*

Nearly all the children volunteer the fact that they do not talk to their parents about what they see. The experience of shared viewing is widespread; the experience of shared opinion is very rare.

When children watch television they are listening to what it says and seeing what it shows. To talk about it would demand more concentration and control than children feel television warrants. The condition of watching television is such that there is no reason why they should not talk at the same time as viewing, and talk specifically about what they see, although the television cannot be interrupted. But the evidence suggests that remarks that are made about the news on television are not analytical but rather attitudinal: 'Silly fools', 'There they go again', 'That wretched man', 'Isn't it awful?' What is being presented to children, therefore, is a series of reflections on the news items rather than any detailed explanation of the issues. Long before any analysis of political and social issues is made, certain postures and reactions become automatic. Some of these are obvious — 'how shocking!' Others are reflex habits on which later opinions are based.

The children recognized that they did not talk much about what they saw on television. When they were asked for more details they were adamant that talking with parents or others very rarely happened, even in isolated incidents. Instead of interested concern with particular items children remembered overhearing general reactions.

> 'My father talks about it. Natter, natter, natter . . . I talk with my brother.' *(girl, 9)*

> 'My parents watch the news. Well, try and ask questions but they always want to listen so I have to wait until the end. Well, I'm very interested in the stars and the planets.' *(girl, 9)*

There are, pointedly, two exceptions:

> 'We talk because my brother's older and my parents are kind of trying to make us have our own ideas about things.' *(girl, 10)*

> 'If I don't understand something I ask her and Daddy. I usually ask Daddy.' *(girl, 10)*

Sustained talk about what is on television is rare. Although children can carry on all kinds of other activities whilst the television is on, such as doing homework and entertaining, the actual watching of the screen is accepted as something almost private. One might watch the television but not talk about it. It is important to convey the fact that the rapidity of the editing, and the continual flow of items, means that it is difficult to isolate particular events or details. Most children watch television with their parents, but that does not mean that the condition of viewing is different from those who watch by themselves, or with their friends or siblings. But whether they watch by themselves or with others, the television does not elicit lengthy discussion. 'It depends who's in the room.' What is absorbed from television is a series of images, and pictures of the world.

Children's attitudes towards authority reveal how much they depend on images that are akin to those seen on the television.[11] There is a combination of acceptance that there is bound to be a conflict between different people, each of whom wishes to present, in a public way, their own point of view. Arguments between politicians who revile each other, as well as a series of negative criticisms, together with shots designed to have the maximum visual impact, give a distinct tone to what is perceived. When children talk about the news they see on television it is possible to see some of the relationships between their developing points of view and the information on which it is based. This is not to suggest that they take in all the information they receive. On the contrary, most of it is very rapidly forgotten. Instead children see the world in terms of the salience of particular stories, and in the relationships between one story and another which accumulate into an overall picture. Their view of the news is casual and pictorial, accumulative rather than analytic.

The view of the world presented through the news is vivid and sensational in a way we have grown accustomed to take for granted. We all know the potency of those items of news which we have heard through word of mouth; on holiday, perhaps. This contrasts with the more mundane spectacle of headlines, of the same number of news items whether anything significant has happened or not, with headlines in the same bold type whether concerned with an assassination or, 'Whew, what a scorcher!' And yet such designs on viewers' responses does not have the effect of causing deep interest in children. One might have thought that the televised news would be considered harmful for the innocent reactions of young children, but only one boy's parents considered that, 'There's too many nasty things on it . . . parents don't approve of it.' (boy, 9). This boy, however, demonstrated an extensive awareness of all the 'nasty things' on the news.

The series of headlines, pictures and strongly held opinions which make up the news, with sound bites and the dominance of the pictorial, precludes analysis. The stories are without background, without explanations of their context. It is this background that children have to fill in for themselves, sometimes through guesswork, and sometimes with a little help from parents and friends. It is no surprise, therefore, that what children remember of the news consists of headlines. They take in the raw information and rarely analyse it, at least at first or deliberately. It is partly because of the passive way that news programmes and documentaries are received that they find them dull. Rarely are issues presented that demand some kind of responsive engagement.

> 'I think it's rather boring, some of the things, but some of the things I just ask questions . . . like petitions for stopping animals suffering and . . . um . . . old people to get more money for their homes and such.' *(girl, 9)*

But there are few matters that engage their sympathies or evoke their interest. They have seen which items are significant in universal terms, but even these come and go. They will recognize what they have seen rather than recall it. And even the most spectacular items of the moment — the blowing up of a United States space shuttle, famine in Ethiopia or the Iraqi invasion of Kuwait — soon become history. It is the type of event that remains in the mind: war; starvation; suffering and disasters.

Given the number of news items which appear, most of them fleetingly, and given the conditions in which children watch television, it is no surprise that much of what is seen is immediately forgotten.

> 'There's lots of worrying things on the news. You can't really pick out in particular; 'cos there's lots of things in the world . . . IRA . . . bicycle cases . . .' *(boy, 9)*

The children were asked to recall any particularly significant or important item that they had seen on the news or read about in newspapers. All the children viewed news as something seen on television, rather than being read or talked about. A significant number of children responded immediately by saying that they couldn't remember anything. Despite having seen a constant flow of news items they did not associate their experience with any sense of order, as if what was seen on television somehow was not worth paying close attention to, and wasn't a subject for discussion. They would say:

> 'I watch it all the time.'

27

but find it difficult to recollect even the headlines.

> 'I think it's quite good actually . . . can't remember anything.' *(girl, 10)*

> 'Um, I'm trying to think of last night on *Coast to Coast*, but I can't think of much.' *(boy, 9)*

Not bothering to recall things seen on television is partly due to the lack of desire to do so, to spend energy on thinking about it. But such a lack of willingness is only associated with television, not with attitudes children hold towards the law, the government or the police. The television images stream past without analysis.

When children receive a series of images which they cannot all recall they are left with associations, and a lack of surprise at all the pictures of violence. They will recognize the same pictures if they see them again but will not be able to delineate their significance.

> 'I don't take much notice of it . . . we usually have tea while we watch the news.' *(girl, 10)*

Not being able, or willing, to recall any particular item does not mean that no impression has been made, but that it has become part of the patina of entertainment. The items that children recollect as subjects remain vague, like 'war', 'crashes' and 'explosions'. Items remain part of an inventory of attitudes rather than the construction of clear principles. There are so many levels of news, from general disasters to domestic, humorous stories, and so many different and contrasting stories that children find it difficult to pick out one.

> 'Ethiopia . . . about trains crashing.' *(girl, 7)*

> 'There's wildlife conservation and teachers . . . striking.' *(boy, 10)*

> 'About missiles . . . Ethiopia.' *(girl, 8)*

> 'I've seen the Shuttle, Libya, Pakistan and Iraq.' *(boy, 10)*

Children have almost too much to choose from, from a series of international disasters to a succession of stories of violence in the UK.

In many children's eyes, the stories that appear in the news are generally about violence, from riots to the suffering caused by natural disasters. The very vagueness of their response is due to the succession of spectacular, accumulative events around which the news is built.

'Lots of things . . . the riots . . . bad.' *(girl, 8)*

'The crashes . . . and lately I've seen a train that crashed.' *(boy, 7)*

Each specific incident is part of a general pattern, of repeated and similar problems and disasters:

'Kidnapping . . . all the murders of the world and everything.' *(boy, 10)*

'People killing other people.' *(boy, 10)*

'Well, all it takes is one person to start a riot . . . all these children keep disappearing all the time.' *(boy, 11)*

'They've been shooting people, the guerrillas and that.' *(girl, 10)*

'People dying . . . starvation and drought.' *(boy, 8)*

Television sees itself as a cheerful medium, with fast-moving images, plenty of entertainment and slick editing. But in the news, television cheerfully conveys all that goes wrong, especially in the spectacular short term. Whatever the tone of the presentation, the catalogue of woes can easily give the impression of a bleak world. The underlying association of news with violence comes about because of the stories which connect with each other and which children understand as a pattern which reflects human nature. They recall examples of a general trend.

'I like serious things about murdering. It's more interesting than burgling.' *(girl, 8)*

The example of this 'serious' and 'interesting' thing is one that could be related to her own environment.

'Well, when they got Maya and when a little girl called Heidi, her father locked her up in a room because she had nicked something like a sweet. So he locked her up in there and she didn't want to come out.' *(girl, 8)*

Out of the many items of news certain specific details stand out, sometimes because they are typical, sometimes because they are spectacular and sometimes because it is possible to imagine them taking place close to home.

'Well, I've heard about the teachers' strike coming to an end . . .
about Northern Ireland and Southern Ireland and riots and things . . .
I heard about this man who got more than £17,000 compensation for
. . . in riots . . . have a paving slab dropped on his back.' *(boy, 10)*

'That lady with that baby. She got threatened . . . um, Punks and that
. . . kill the baby because they said . . . the police said to her that she
shouldn't have married a black man . . . anyway, so the baby's black.'
(girl, 9)

Children can be very confused in relating what they have seen. This
is partly because of the way in which the stories are presented.
Headlines draw attention to a particular point; the highlights, the
result of action, always precede the explanation, the build-up or
the cause. Particular impressions stand out vividly. Instead of a
coherent story, it is the details that remain potent.

'The 6-year-old girl that was going to school and she got kidnapped by
this man in a taxi.' *(boy, 9)*

'The vicar's daughter that was raped . . . the swans being
cleaned.' *(girl, 9)*

'I remember the Putney gas explosion and the Brighton bombing . . .
the miners' strike.' *(boy, 8)*

A lot depends on the pictures that they have seen:

'The bombs that are exploding. Ethiopia, that's sorry, because they're
starving. When you . . . pictures . . . they're very thin and they've got
flies all over them.' *(boy, 8)*

The images that are experienced on television might not always be
understood but they nevertheless contain an impact which remains.
Children accumulate a number of different facts, a mixture of items
that stay in their minds for different reasons, sometimes because
they connect to their own experience, real or imagined, and sometimes because the impression being given is so clear. Many children
present a number of examples of how heterogeneous the images are
that the television presents:

'I think all the fighting in South Africa is horrible and the cricketer who
walked to Land's End raising money for leukaemia.' *(boy, 9)*

'Umm . . . I remember one thing that I saw that the Pope went to see
Mother Theresa and on *Newsround* there was something about a panda

and this . . . on *Coast to Coast* there was this lady and her husband left her an hour after the service.' *(girl, 10)*

Some of the incidents that children remember are the spectacularly violent ones; others are stories that have interested or frightened them, perhaps because they can imagine being in the same circumstances.

'About someone who went sledging and they died because they went into a tree . . . Germany had a big car crash . . . the Ethiopians, lots of them have died of hunger.' *(boy, 8)*

'Some people are dying in Spain. Elderly people. They've found some new food for pandas . . .' *(girl, 9)*

The most spectacular images clearly make an impact. The really large news items, especially if often repeated and discussed as they unfold, or when they are anticipated, will be likely to remain in their minds. But children will also be interested in news items which are closer to home, and which have a bearing on their own lives and where they live. The journalists' adage that one death next door is equal in interest to one thousand deaths abroad, is borne out in the way that children discuss the news. There are only a small number of items which demand their attention — stories which are repeated day after day, stories which are spectacular and stories which connect with their own immediate experience. Children do not weigh the significance of the news. They react according to the item's particular impact, but they also internalize what they see to make sense out of it. Some items trigger their interest, even if they are of no great universal significance.

'Once I saw a girl who had a dog. It was a stray dog. It was telling you that it would have to be put down if it wasn't claimed in two days.' *(girl, 8)*

Domestic details or human-interest stories are a part of their memory, as they are part of the material that makes up the daily pattern of news.

'There's the polar bear that's learned to do tricks and the Government is having rows.' *(girl, 9)*

'About aeroplanes. The people who used to have them in the air. In the Air Force . . . and they came back to fly them [Spitfires] some of them did.' *(girl, 11)*

'About the RSPCA, well, they're stopping people from hurting animals and that . . . Because they haven't got enough money and they think animals . . . they can just have . . . but, you know, not look after them.' *(girl, 9)*

Human-interest stories are designed to make an impact on the audience, to manipulate feelings of sentimentality or pathos. But they also play a part in revealing a world in which children or animals can suffer. Whilst the most spectacular happenings will almost inevitably come from far away, there is nearly always a sense in which it *could* happen here. But children do not simply dismiss all that they see as irrelevant. It might not be interesting to them but the news gives a picture of the world that is the most comprehensive they receive. Although they themselves are not actual witnesses to riots, or wars or starvation, children see these news stories as examples of what people do. Some of the problems *could*, after all, be close to home:

'Well, I'm not too pleased because we were going to move one of our great-aunts to one of the places which had just had a riot. We had already decided and she had just gone in a few days and then there were riots in that town. So they've moved her to a different home.' *(boy, 9)*

The items of news which make the most impact have certain ingredients in common: the human interest, and the spectacular picture, together with attention repeated over several days so that people wonder what will happen next. A space-shuttle disaster has all the ingredients to cause a major, if temporary, impact. It is shown live on television: the shots are clear and often repeated, it is spectacular, it has a great deal of human response bound in it, and the recriminations continue for several days.

'About the rocket that blew up. And all the tragedies that they have been facing. And that poor teacher who died in it.' *(girl, 10)*

'The Shuttle Changer exploding. The last shuttle. The last Challenger one. The people that were in it . . . it didn't explode. They were putting some rubber wiring round it and they said, "That's no good," because they already had some there in the first place. It was inside at the back . . . around inside in the bits . . . they were going to put it on the outside and the inside.' *(boy, 10)*

There are some news items which one can be sure that the children will know about, even if they are not the first to be recalled. But it proves how children assiduously watch the news, however reluctantly or indifferently. A spectacular public event, like the explosion of the spacecraft, is bound to be taken in and, if not analysed, at least reacted to.

'Well, I was interested when the space shuttle you know, blew up.' *(boy, 11)*

'The shuttle and stuff like that. It was a bit disastrous, the worse so far.' *(boy, 10)*

'The shuttle disaster. It was awful. They were just getting ready for a decent day and it came and blew up.' *(girl, 11)*

'About the shuttle explosion. It was terrible . . . the teacher.' *(girl, 10)*

In defining the salience given to an item of news, one of the ingredients which makes it significant is not just the spectacular nature but the amount of attention that it sustains over several days. This attention is given not so much to the event itself, however often repeated, but to the discussion of the event. Whilst children are aware of the significant natural disasters around the world, they do not think of them as more important news items than political storms at home. This is not just because of the pictorial nature of television, but because the easiest images to acquire are those of people talking about what has happened. To avoid too much of the newsreaders talking to camera, producers turn to short interviews — sound bites to create a faster-moving sequence of images. Thus children acquire an image of politicians as people who are either bound up by the news, or blaming others for what has happened. An item of news sustains interest by being discussed, by being referred to repeatedly. Political arguments, especially between members of the Cabinet, become important news items in the eyes of children, not necessarily because of the issues discussed, but because of their presentation of the nature of human affairs. Politicians lay blame. They defend themselves from blame. Things are going wrong. It is someone's fault. The only question is, whose? One sometimes gets the impression that children hear the accusations given by one political party about another, and vice versa, about their failures, stupidities and moral limitations, and believe *both* of them.

Children receive a great deal of information about the world they live in. This information is mediated only to a limited extent by the presenters of information, the 'gatekeepers', and their families and friends. Children have to make sense of a mass of raw data, not self-consciously or deliberately, but as a way of coping with it. They need to learn how to digest what they see on the news, how to approach it. It is for this reason that they retain general 'slots' into which they can place what they see: 'riots' or 'disasters' or 'animal stories'. They also form opinions of what they see: 'I used to be bored [with the news] but I'm quite interested now.' (girl, 10). They react very strongly to some politicians, especially the Prime Minister, and are interested in the ubiquitous Royal Family. Their opinions of Mrs Thatcher were based on an awareness that she evoked particular reactions, not just in themselves or perhaps their parents, but in others:

> 'People say Maggie Thatcher ought to give up being leader of, I think it's the Conservative Party.' *(girl, 9)*

> 'People making rude remarks about her, like *Spitting Image*, to make people laugh.' *(girl, 9)*

Above all, children become aware of the weight of a variety of opinions. The world is not just full of facts, but of *causes*.

> 'The Government, because there are things where people are staying in flats and things like that and their flats aren't very good. They're damp and yukky. I saw that on the news once.' *(girl, 10)*

When any issue is explored with children it becomes clear that they will have *some* kind of opinion about it, proving that they have received information, from various sources, and proving that they are aware of a continuing debate. The case of the Channel Tunnel demonstrates this. Children might be indifferent to the news, but know what is taking place, and are aware of the arguments involved — the debating points made by commercial interests. But they also have their own personal reactions to the realities of a tunnel.

> 'Well, I don't like trains. But there are some people, they have to get there quicker and if you sort of go on things like the ferry, it takes absolutely hours. I've experienced that. And the hovercraft is faster but it doesn't necessarily take you.' *(girl, 10)*

Many children project themselves into the possibilities of a disaster; they generally reveal a fairly negative opinion of the Channel Tunnel, for one reason or another.

'If there's a leak and it suddenly gets really big then, if it all goes, then loads of people would die and they'll have to build it all over again.' *(boy, 11)*

'Because, I mean, if there was a leak or something, well, also if there's a big queue and you're stuck in there for hours, no daylight or anything . . . nothing can be done.'   *(girl, 11)*

The sense of potential disaster in the tunnel does not arise only because of a sense of claustrophobia, or a lack of wholehearted belief in the processes of technology. Children have been attuned to the prevalence of terrorism: the tunnel might collapse, not through natural causes, but unnatural ones.

'Well, as it said on the news, it takes just one silly person to blow it up and it would be chaos.'   *(boy, 10)*

'I'd be scared of people bombing it.'   *(girl, 9)*

'Hoaxers and people could just say, "I've put a bomb on the train," and they'd have to evacuate the whole train and the whole tunnel.' *(boy, 10)*

The children's reactions to the Channel Tunnel reflect some of the ancient debates about the islands of Great Britain and the importance of the English Channel as a barrier against invasion, of one kind or another.

'Well, if we had a war or anything . . . well, we can easily blow up the tunnel but I prefer England just to be by itself. I don't like the idea of foreigners coming in everywhere.'   *(girl, 9)*

Awareness of world-wide issues does not necessarily mean a shift in chauvinism. But the children also fear another kind of invasion, aware as they are of the issue of rabies.

'Because there's diseases in France and they'll probably get to England. If any rats come across in the tunnel they could easily spread diseases.'   *(girl, 10)*

'Because if they're going to have air ventilators they could bring rabies and other diseases to animals in this country.'   *(boy, 11)*

'It might bring rabies into Britain and, as well, lots of French apples and French things . . . but nothing can be done.' *(girl, 10)*

It is not only spectacular events that make their impact. Children are all aware of continuing issues, even if they do not construct a deliberate point of view about them. But connections are made between one event and another. Images of the world outside are unavoidable. But this does not make them necessarily less parochial.[12] They are aware of their own environment, and the difference between events which affect them, and those that can safely remain items of less interest. Thus there remains a certain suspicion of the rest of the world, a parochialism which seems unaffected by living, through the eyes of broadcasting, in a 'global village'. The way in which pictures of the world are presented, and how children respond to them, shows how isolated and incoherent much of the material remains. The pictures that are presented about Africa, for example, tend to be of war and starvation; of poverty and aridity.[13] Children do not always know where the countries are, or the political background to the news, but they are fed many images and all know about Ethiopia because of the television campaigns that have drawn attention to it. Within all the significant items of news emerge images of Africa.

'I mean about 100 people dying in Africa . . . it's terrible and nobody seems to be doing anything about it.' *(girl, 9)*

'The Ethiopians, they spent all their money on weapons and things and didn't spend enough on food and things.' *(boy, 8)*

Children might reveal that their analysis of what is happening is not complex or sophisticated, but neither is it cool and unaffected. Children hold views and strong feelings about issues, be they the Channel Tunnel or Africa. The images they receive might not enter a carefully formed intellectual 'set', but they become part of their coherent emotional life. The issues *matter* to them.

'I think it's the Ethiopian people. Because there's a war on as well, and so the other people are not quite sure who they are fighting, and they are bashing their homes up, and so they might lose their money or something, and so they haven't got any clothes or anything and they're starving now.' *(girl, 9)*

'The starving people in Ethiopia; that's the worst thing I've heard of . . . Did you hear on the news once when they said that the Government was against itself raising money for Ethiopia?' *(girl, 7)*

Current events, including political issues as well as international incidents, present themselves on television as being emotionally highly charged. A sophisticated audience can learn the studied indifference to events that are of no immediate concern. But children receive a series of strongly held and argued views, from politicians about each other, and from journalists about politicians. Rather than responding with an overall political or diplomatic analysis of what they see, children create a network of emotional attitudes. What they see matters to them. They feel there should be some action in response to events. But, in the end, the pictures they receive do not remain specific to certain places and certain events. The news, and reactions to the news, become generalized. The most important events on the news tend to be the same ones.

'Kidnapping, all the murders in the world and everything.' *(boy, 10)*

'Earthquakes and things . . . other things like murders and things like that.' *(girl, 10)*

'About all the accidents. About their still pulling people from the rubble and all that.' *(boy, 10)*

Children's views of the society in which they live are being formed and developed from an early age. These views, as the evidence of the following chapters reveals, are strongly held, emotionally charged and coherent. And yet children are developing their views with little formal help. They do not often discuss current affairs with their teachers. Teachers are, indeed, discouraged from dealing with 'political' issues, like peace. Dialogue of any length with parents is rare. Television presents images to an audience that is busy doing other things at the same time as observing them. And yet children find enough sources of information to form their views about a variety of issues, parochial and international. They share these views with each other, showing how much of the time they are engaged, privately, in trying to puzzle out reasons for what happens. But in all this television plays an important and symbolic role. It is the most potent source of information, both in the strength of its pictures and the amount of time it is watched. It is also viewed as a window in the world; a window that lets light in but is often ignored, but a window whose outlook becomes hauntingly familiar.

NOTES AND REFERENCES

1. Cullingford, C. *The Inner World of the School*. London: Cassell, 1991.
2. Short, J., Williams, E., and Christie, B. *The Social Psychology of Telecommunications*. London: Wiley, 1976.
3. Katz, E., and Lazarsfeld, P. F. *Personal Influence: The Part Played by People in the Flow of Mass Communications*. Glencoe, IL: Free Press, 1955.
4. Kapferer, Jean-Noel. *Rumeurs. Le plus vieux media du monde*. Paris: Editions du Seuil, 1987.
5. Sabini, J., and Silver, M. *Moralities of Everyday Life*. New York: Oxford University Press, 1982.
6. Newcomb, T. M. 'An approach to the study of communication acts.' *Psychological Review*, **60**, 393–404, 1953.
7. Cullingford, C. *Children and Television*. Aldershot: Gower, 1984.
8. Jaros, D., and Kelson, V. L. 'The multifarious leader: political socialisation of Amish, ''Yanks'' and ''Blacks''.' In R. Niemi (ed.), *The Politics of Future Citizens*. London: Jossey Bass, 1974.
9. *Ibid*.
10. Newcomb, T. M., *op. cit*.
11. See later chapters.
12. Cullingford, C. 'The parochial and the ethnocentric: children's attitudes to other countries.' *Education 3–13*, **18**(2), 29–34, 1990.
13. Graham, J., and Lynn, S. 'Mud huts and flints: children's images of the Third World.' *Education 3–13*, **17**(2), 29–32, 1989.

CHAPTER 4

The Individual and the World of Politics

'I think that somewhere there's a politician that I like but I've never found one yet.' *(boy, 8)*

Socrates saw politics as the manifestation of articulate social life. Today we associate the term not so much with the art of govern-ment as with internecine strife, limited to a minority of interested parties. Such a narrowing of the conception of politics which allows impossible statements such as, 'I am not interested in politics', partly explains how little interest is shown in how children acquire their own individual, and political, points of view. Both in the broad sense and even in the narrowest party-political terms, chil-dren observe political actions, statements and consequences every day.

Many of their observations derive from television. It might not have made children more articulate about politics, but it has ensured that they see politics in action.[1] Television has insured that children receive a wealth of information even if it rarely deals with political attitudes.[2] Children are passive observers who are used to seeing things presented to them. They observe a world in which they play no active part. It is like a world complete in itself in which other people are protagonists, others make the decisions. The con-sequences of decisions, and the blame for decisions are constantly presented. Children become accustomed to a passive role but they also accept that nearly all that they see is due to someone's mistake, or some ill-intentioned action. They receive information. Much of it is concerned with accidents and disasters. And after the hard news follow the recriminations.

Children therefore observe passionate opinions, and develop strong emotional reactions to what they see. And whilst they can do nothing they are nevertheless taught to think that *something* should be done, *someone* should act. Whilst they might be passive viewers, they associate political events with immediate action. Actions are more significant than issues. So children learn about the power of politicians, those who *could* act, as well as the pervasive nature of politics.

Children also observe the power of authority and government in their own schools. They are treated to a display of everyday politics in action, in the authority of the headteacher, the importance of collective decisions, the power of outsiders, like governors, and the individuality of each teacher's actions. The sense of order runs deep in children. Their early experiences of learning are attempts to place the complexities of what is seen into a coherent structure. They do not wish to simplify as some professional politicians might wish to simplify, but they do need to know how to fit new information into their own points of view. Much early learning is the placing of experience into a pattern of understanding. Order is essential. But order is not just a matter of understanding. It is a matter of behaviour. The need to know what is expected of them at home, consistently and firmly, is then reflected in the order of the school. Children like to know exactly how the rules work, and respect the teacher who maintains authority.[3]

Schools are seen by children as being hierarchical places in which some people carry more authority than others. Adults generally, and essentially, carry more authority than children, and yet children rate the authority of their peers more highly than that of adults they do not respect.[4] They analyse not just the kind of command given but the social position of those giving it. Thus it is those who assume authority, by the nature of their position rather than age, who carry most weight. The headteacher is clearly seen by children as the most important person in the school, even if their personal contact with her is comparatively slight. Children know how a school works.

Children realize that the headteacher is not in complete isolation. There are others who are involved in the running of the school, like 'governors', 'people at Shire Hall', 'The Ministry', 'the teaching unions, things like that'. Sometimes one particular individual looms behind the headteacher.

'I think she [the headteacher] asks the one who asked her to be head-teacher. The one who lives up at the top. She's the one that sort of owns the school. Lady E., they call her.' *(girl, 9)*

The relationship between teachers and the head is manifest in the school; but children know about the larger politics that affect the running of the school.

At the same time as recognizing the authority of the headteacher children realize that most decisions are discussed with others, within or outside the school:

> 'Mrs H. discusses things with other people.' *(girl, 11)*
>
> 'I should think she talks to the other teachers to see if they agree with her.' *(girl, 11)*
>
> 'She decides by herself but some she discusses with Mrs L. and Mr H.' *(boy, 10)*
>
> 'He goes to meetings and discusses it.' *(boy, 10)*

There is no sense of a simple dictatorship of the head. Children yearn for order and authority. But they know that it needs to be achieved. They know it depends on acceptance. Behind school rules, as behind laws, lie a series of discussions.

> 'I think when the parents and the governors get together they all discuss it and talk about it and then they get some final rules that they say . . .' *(girl, 10)*

Children in school accept the need for clear rules and demand that they should be fairly and firmly implemented. But they are also aware that authority depends on some kind of consensus, and that a hierarchy of power invested in the headteacher and others is, in fact, surrounded by a lot of discussion and negotiation.

Children, then, experience actual politics in the running of their schools, and observe the outcomes of politics on television. How does this equip them to understand how governments and societies interact? The combination of observation and information leads children to conclude that the position of the Prime Minister is all important. Media coverage ensured that Mrs Thatcher was by far the best-known politician at the time this study was done; all the children knew her name. Whilst they might be more vague about how government generally functions, they did recognize the Prime Minister's dominant role. Number 10 Downing Street was better known to them than the Houses of Parliament. The Cabinet was seen as a group of advisers who served a dominating Prime Minister. Rules and decisions were seen to emanate from her. Children acknowledged that they were aware of her since she appeared so often on television, citing her usually as Margaret Thatcher rather than 'Maggie' or 'Mrs Thatcher'. The collective role of government was less easy to define. Whilst they accepted that the Prime Minister took advice, they had a clear sense that it was she who made the decisions.

> 'Mrs Thatcher. Just talking, telling everybody what to do and that sort of thing.' *(boy, 9)*

> 'Even though I don't like her, she's very powerful in Britain.' *(girl, 7)*

The sense of a balance between one dominant personality and a vague hinterland of advice is a theme that pervades all analyses of government. It is echoed in a similar balance between the sense of majority decisions and having to submit to what has been decided.

> 'The Prime Minister . . . they have lots of discussions and things but I think she makes some rules that other people don't agree with but the majority of people do and so the people who don't agree just have to put up with it.' *(girl, 10)*

There is a tendency, shared by adults, for children to see power in personal terms, invested in the President or Prime Minister. This does not mean that they see these figures as exemplars of good behaviour, but they do grow accustomed to accepting the authority of central figures. It is as if people become part of the status quo. They might be viewed with a jaundiced eye, but they represent society as it is.[5]

The children were clear about Mrs Thatcher's central importance, and they knew her name. By the age of 7 children know about conceptions of power and rules.[6] But they are less clear about titles and job descriptions. The idea of a President, so often referred to on television, could confuse them.

> 'Oh . . . mm, what's it called, umm, the President, I think, or something like that . . . Margaret Thatcher.' *(girl, 10)*

> 'Margaret Thatcher . . . She's the President of the country.' *(boy, 8)*

But they were in no doubt about her name and personality.

> 'Mrs Thatcher. She's the President. Well, she's on the news sometimes. She travels from country to country.' *(boy, 8)*

They were also aware of the power of the role, whether they see it as temporary — 'The Prime Minister who is in power at the moment. That's Mrs Thatcher.' *(girl, 11)* — or as something seemingly more permanent — 'Margaret Thatcher. She runs the world. I think she does it by herself.' *(girl, 10)*.

It is, of course, difficult to separate the person from the position. The way that the Prime Minister is presented, whether through party political broadcasts, or the news, is as a familiar figure, taking photo opportunities as well as making speeches. This led children into the occasional muddle between the Prime Minister and the Queen.

'Margaret Thatcher . . . She's the Queen of England.' *(boy, 11)*

'She's Prime Minister because she helps people. She's part of the Royal Family.' *(girl, 9)*

Such lapses were, however, rare. Even when she was merged into an enlarged Royal Family, her name was known, together with the fact that she carried power. Public figures of that kind are, after all, supposed to be political symbols as well as personalities, focal points for loyalty, like the Queen.[7]

The few children who confused the constitutional positions of the Prime Minister and the Queen were revealing at the same time their awareness of the collective nature of a government. The Prime Minister was dominant but not isolated. Around her were a host of advisers who listened to her. She 'has other people to talk to' or 'talks to the Government and she talks to the Queen'. Thus a sense that people other than the Prime Minister can occasionally make decisions (rare as this is in the eyes of children) tends to focus on the other major, and permanent, public figure.

'The Government makes most of the decisions. Sometimes the Queen makes decisions.' *(boy, 10)*

The impression that the Prime Minister is not alone is to some extent a visual one. Whilst the centre of attention, Mrs Thatcher was nevertheless surrounded by a coterie who must have some kind of function. Television images include an array of other people:

'She has . . . she used to have somebody, er, what's the name. She has a secretary and people who go around with her. Bodyguards.' *(girl, 9)*

'With other people. Her husband and the people who work for her.'
(girl, 9)

The impression children received of the Prime Minister was of someone always talking, but they saw this as a natural function of her job rather than characteristic of her personality. She had to give speeches and interviews. But she had also to talk to all those who surrounded her and whom she visited:

'She's got other people. They help her with her work. And they sign her up for trips and things she has to go on. Sometimes she goes and sees the poor people. Or sometimes she just goes to see the Prime Minister of America. I think she talks about all the things that are going on in England and he most probably talks about the things that are going on in America.' *(girl, 10)*

The speeches that she made were often seen in the context of Parliament, so that there was a growing awareness of other people having a place in government:

'She makes speeches, things like that. I think she talks to other people, Members of Parliament.' *(girl, 11)*

'I think she has other people; MPs. Some helpful, some not.'
(boy, 10)

The other people who surrounded the Prime Minister were seen as being there to 'help her'. She received advice and support, from advisers, from MPs and the Cabinet.

'I expect she has help from other people. Other Presidents and special and famous people.' *(girl, 10)*

The 'other people' were seen as playing minor roles but being in the position of giving advice because of their own importance.

'She decides about things, what are going on in the country. Other MPs help.' *(boy, 11)*

It was, however, clear that in the tension between the authority of the Prime Minister and her advisers, it is the Prime Minister who made decisions.

'Everything that comes up, she's in charge of it . . . She discusses it with other people.' *(boy, 8)*

Children's apprehension of the significance of central personalities does not mean that they are unaware that the constitution, including Parliament, involves many people, however highlighted particular people are. They know that surrounding her position is some kind of support in a collective will — 'She has votes and that'. But there is also an awareness of the party system. This manifests itself, significantly enough, in their awareness of the Labour party. The Conservative party being the one in power is presented on the media as the Government. When party differences are highlighted it is the Labour party that is recalled. This can lead to some curious cross-references. If Mrs Thatcher dominated the Government, and the Labour party is the symbol of the voting system, it explains why some children associated the two.

> 'She helps the Labour party. They sort out things. Seen them on telly.' *(girl, 8)*

> 'Well it's either Labour or the Government. The Government makes most of the decisions.' *(boy, 10)*

> 'She's the Prime Minister. Works for Labour.' *(girl, 8)*

More children assumed that Mrs Thatcher worked for Labour than mentioned the Conservative party. One even suggested where her advice came from:

> 'She has other people, Neil Kinnock and that.' *(boy, 9)*

But the analysis of the relationship between government and party rarely goes very deep. There is only the occasional hint of party politics, and then for clear reasons.

> 'Maggie Thatcher. She leads our party and tries to work things out and the leaders of the groups.' *(boy, 11)*

The functions of government and the nature of the constitution do not form part of the curriculum in a democratic country. By the time young people vote they will have had to make sense of the workings of society in their own way, seeking information from a variety of sources. The easiest aspects of government to understand are the most visible of facts: the Prime Minister and Parliament. These facts children of 8 or so have no difficulty with; they usually know the name of the Prime Minister and know about the House of Lords. But few know about the actual working of government.

There are certain things, after all, that remain secret and obscure to the whole of the electorate. So children had difficulty in ascertaining what Mrs Thatcher actually did as Prime Minister, how she spent her time and what she was responsible for. The comments that they made reflect some of the images that are presented of certain kinds of action, whatever these actions are for:

> 'She talks to the presidents when she goes to different countries.' *(boy, 8)*

> 'She gives sort of speeches and that. She makes sure everything is sort of OK.' *(girl, 10)*

The image presented was of someone who was always talking, in meetings or to the general public, talking to present ideas rather than exchange them.

> 'She holds speeches and that . . . She decides everything by herself.' *(boy, 8)*

The children give the impression that Mrs Thatcher had endless meetings; ' . . . mostly in meetings, talking to people.' (boy, 7), meetings which include a certain amount of arguing: 'Really they argue over things. About the country.' (girl, 10). But they are clear about why there is a need for so many meetings. The Prime Minister was there to act, to put things right concerning:

> 'Anything that's important, really. Like things to do with planes and food and clothes and all the important things that we need to live with.' *(boy, 9)*

It is out of these meetings that the rules are laid down, that laws are made.

> 'It's all about ruling the country. I'm not sure what else they talk about. Oh, yes, they make new rules.' *(girl, 10)*

The Prime Minister was both spokeswoman and legislator; meeting with people to form policies:

> 'Well if there are things that are wrong, she bans them. She's a law thing. She probably consults other people as well.' *(girl, 11)*

Given the symbolic function of the position, and the power invested in it, it is not surprising that children have high expectations of what the Prime Minister is capable of. Mrs Thatcher was there to do good. Children have always had a tendency to think of political figures as benevolent, despite television.[8] This is part of a natural desire to see the world as ordered and justified: public figures are presented with a sense of virtue, despite all the criticism that they face. The Prime Minister, therefore, spent her time trying to make the world a better place.

> 'How to make things more enjoyable for us and how to share things more equally.' *(girl, 9)*

> 'Margaret Thatcher talks about getting people from the rubble and working and all that; stop violence and all that . . . petrol bombs and all that . . . they've made kinds of shields for the men.' *(boy, 10)*

Such a range of powers shows how far Mrs Thatcher was seen to be in control. This is part of the sense that the government as a whole is largely subsumed within one individual. Parliament as a power is rarely mentioned. The begetter and presenter of the Government is the Prime Minister. She does the explaining and cajoling, has the meetings and makes the decisions.

Such a range of potential powers did not necessarily make the Prime Minister popular. On the one hand:

> 'Maggie Thatcher makes sure everything's under order and helps pensioners and children's work, and the unemployed . . . and all those sort of things.' *(girl, 11)*

On the other hand such high expectations of the power to keep 'everything in order' leads to disillusionment:

> 'I don't think Margaret Thatcher is doing a very good job of it. She's only making all the money for herself. She's not giving it to the people who need it.' *(girl, 9)*

There was a general tendency for young people to express an antipathy to Mrs Thatcher.[9] But children do not express themselves generally in vehement terms. Signs of attacking her on political or personal grounds were rare. They were far more objective. They understood her personal style and the way she was presented, but they also understood the importance of her *position*. Their observations led them to believe that other Prime Ministers would have similar effects. After all, she could lose office:

'Well, I think we're going to be losing Mrs Thatcher quite soon because as she's getting older she could get defeated in time. Then a new government would come in.' *(boy, 10)*

The power that surrounds the Prime Minister is due to the function of office, as part of the system of government. Obviously the way such power is presented is a matter of style — 'a big decision-maker, like Mrs Thatcher' — *(boy, 10)*, but the essential point is that a single person holds power. This is both symbolic and real. It is symbolic because the Prime Minister's power lies at the apex of a hierarchy: she expresses a collective will. Children see the Prime Minister standing for the whole government. In Brecht's *Galileo* the narrator points out to the audience how historians use phrases such as 'Alexander the Great conquered the East', 'Julius Caesar invaded Britain'. He then ponders the facts. 'Alone?', asks the narrator. 'Were there no others who helped; horsemen, soldiers . . . no other individuals?' The Prime Minister is seen in that kind of way. But she is also seen to have real power, about which few can do anything.

As head of government, the Prime Minister is seen as the one who makes decisions. Indeed the perception children had of Mrs Thatcher's role suggested that when 'she does the laws' she did so in some detail:

'Never to drink and drive and lots of things like that.' *(girl, 11)*

The question then arises how these decisions are disseminated. Who is it that:

'writes the bills and sends them out . . . the rent of the houses. They decide where roads should be put, provide food and water and play parks.' *(boy, 11)*

This is where the judiciary and some sense of an army of civil servants come into play, to do the detailed work that derives from the many decisions of the Prime Minister. They are aware of the interconnections between the general forces of law and order, the police and the courts, but see them all as deriving from central decisions. Whilst the image of government is focused on one person, the dissemination of decisions is seen to include many people, including judges.

One of the central functions of the administration, in children's eyes, is the raising of revenue through taxes. They know about taxes since this is one of the themes to which politicians keep returning, but are far less clear about the administration of the system.

'Margaret Thatcher gets money from the taxes and then puts it in to help housing. You pay an amount of money every year on every month and it goes into help things.' *(girl, 9)*

'You have to give one-third of that to the government in tax and you keep the rest of the money. What they're spending it on most is weapons and the unemployed. They should spend more on people than in the way of defence.' *(boy, 10)*

That the government imposes taxes is clear; that it spends the money on various activities is also clear:

'Well, if you're very, very rich you have to pay quite a bit more than others who might not be so well off and it is to go towards all the roads and State schools and things like that.' *(girl, 10)*

'Well, it's money that everybody has to pay but you pay less if you haven't got so much money and it goes towards building roads, all sorts of things, hospitals, lots of things.' *(boy, 10)*

It is also clear that children understand the system as a theoretical construct. They are less certain of how the system works:

'A man comes round and collects money from you, like say £10 a week or something like that, and then every four or two weeks, and then they collect all the money up and that's how they get it.' *(boy, 10)*

The sense of a system as a whole remains unclear. Each part of the administration of society is understood: the Cabinet, the judiciary, the collection of revenue. The idea of discussion between interested parties is also conveyed. But the general view is akin to that reflected on television news: of certain people making decisions and having these decisions carried out. This means that the success and failure of systems are directly attributable to individual politicians.

'Some are good. Some are bad. You can't really tell. Some have good policies, some have bad policies.' *(girl, 7)*

The sense of good and bad, clearly defined, is presented clearly by politicians according to their political persuasion. They present the case for the enormity of decisions; how different things would be if the Government hadn't made that mistake, or how magnificent the

Government's performance. The more television highlights central issues, the more obscure the complexities of the Civil Service, local authority and society generally. Sometimes politicians succeed in presenting the case they wish to make with great aplomb. What does the Government achieve?

> 'I think freedom, really. Freedom, most of the time, and jobs. There isn't many jobs now really but I think they do a good job on it . . . of helping people.' *(girl, 10)*

Children note the power of politicians and accept the need for authority. They observe how centrally decisions are made, whilst recognizing that a fair amount of discussion goes into decisions. The question then is whether the individual voices can have any influence and whether the Prime Minister and advisers are responsive to other points of view. The whole question of the individual and the State was explored with the children to see whether they saw themselves as part of a democratic process, how they would communicate their own points of view and whether they had any means of changing things.

Children essentially felt that there was little that any individual could do except submit: 'you just have to put up with it.' Those children who felt that politicians would 'care' were few; and they assumed that they would only be receptive to particular people.

> 'If they know someone and they start telling them what to do, then they might take notice but if they're just normal people then they don't take much notice.' *(boy, 11)*

> 'They do care about rich people. They do care about some people, yes.' *(girl, 8)*

Politicians might present their policies but they do not present themselves as people responsive to the electorate. A few children realize that this might be a problem with how they appear:

> 'Yes, they care. It's just sometimes they don't look as though they care. It just looks like they're interested in their jobs and money.' *(boy, 10)*

The indifference of politicians is, however, not so much a personal thing as a function of their role. They make decisions, and others must put up with them.

'You can't do much because . . . as individuals, unless you've got a strong point you can't really change it.' *(boy, 11)*

The sense that there is nothing significant to be done to change policies, that the individual, unless he or she *knows* politicians personally, is powerless, is all pervasive.

'It's the law and you just have to put up with it.' *(boy, 8)*

'Once the Prime Minister's decided, they can't really do anything about it. They just go their own way really.' *(girl, 10)*

All the children suggested that even if a law were unfair there was little anyone could do. Underlying their responses is the abiding belief that all decisions emanate from the Government, and it is the Government's will that prevails. This does not imply that children feel that every law is sacrosanct. They all accept that some laws are unfair, and some decisions are imposed against the wishes of the majority. Nor do they demonstrate great belief in the wisdom of politicians. Instead, they have an almost cynical belief that the authorities can do what they want, and that citizens are there to put up with the consequences.

However democratically systems work, the sense that laws are imposed to be obeyed, and the sense of the lack of power of the individual, must be part of the effect of any government, at least to a minority. The ordinary individual might not make a difference, but if enough people agree to make a particular point they will make their voice heard. Children go on to point out that even if the voice is heard it will nevertheless be ignored, but they all show enough independence of spirit to be able to disagree with decisions, and say so. They know they *can* protest and they know about voting. Their cynicism about politicians' lack of response is in the context of the right to protest. The idea of protesting, as demonstrated on the news, carries more salience with children than voting; as if they are conscious of making their voice hear about *faits accomplis* rather than changing things. But they know about the power of the majority.

'They can get a gang together to start to stop it. Get votes in and things. And lots of people would vote and they would win.' *(girl, 8)*

'They might be able to, depending on how many votes they get against them having it and how many for.' *(boy, 11)*

51

One way of expressing disagreement with policy in such a way that there might be a change of action is by persuading enough people.

'Not from one person but from a lot of people I think they might take more notice.' *(girl, 10)*

There are a number of ways children suggest in which feelings can be conveyed. The question that remains unanswered in their minds is whether any notice will be taken. Many suggest writing letters, but few imagine any result.

'You just sort of write to Maggie Thatcher, which is what I'd probably do. She might take notice; or put an article in the paper.' *(girl, 10)*

'Well, you could write a letter or they could go to Mrs Thatcher and have a chat with her but that might not change it.' *(boy, 11)*

Nearly all children feel that as decisions begin and end with the Prime Minister, so the only worthwhile person to influence is also her. Only one recognized that a point of view could be expressed to politicians outside the Cabinet.

'Mention it to a Member of Parliament. Though I wouldn't know how to get to one.' *(boy, 10)*

The only real chance of creating change, however, depends on the weight of influence brought to bear.

'I think she'd change her mind if there was a lot of people. I think they should, everybody, um, sort of crowd around her and tell her not to do it.' *(girl, 10)*

Trying to get politicians to respond implies some kind of force. Given the little chance of individual influence children begin to see the right to protest as something valuable in itself. Of course, nothing will happen, but they are aware of demonstrations, petitions, marches, banners, picket lines and riots. A central part of their vision of society is the large crowd protesting in the face of television cameras, controlled by the police. Children accept that a government *ought* to respond. But by government they tend to mean the Prime Minister. And they are aware that protests and demonstrations make little difference, if any. Nevertheless, they are aware of different kinds of protest, conveying equivocal feelings about their efficacy at the same time as recognizing their existence.

'You could do a petition. You have . . . you go round saying to people, if they don't agree with it, they could write their own name down and then you could take it to the Government and show them how many people didn't agree.' *(girl, 10)*

There are also more strenuous and immediate ways of drawing attention to a point of view.

'Protest outside the entrance so that nothing can get through. Marching back and forth so that nothing can get through . . . it won't stop it.' *(girl, 9)*

'Nothing can be done . . . Protest about it . . . go around with banners and sort of write letters . . .' *(boy, 10)*

While children note the possible forms of protest, including the most extreme — 'Fight against the Government; Bombs and that.' *(boy, 10)* — the sense that nothing will result runs like a thread through all their responses. Their equivocation lies in their sense that protest is a waste of time, and therefore almost unseemly. In the end they do not like or approve of all the forms of demonstration they see broadcast. Perhaps if protest worked, then they might approve.

'You could send a letter or telephone them. Well, it's better than protest, because it's asking kindly. It's not going to force them to do it.' *(boy, 11)*

If demonstrations and posters do not do any good, then they see no point in going to all that trouble. After all children are not taught to like riots.

'You should complain to them or something like that but don't go lying in the middle of the road. I'd just say to my Dad how silly it is and sometimes he agrees with me and sometimes he tells me why.' *(boy, 10)*

The problem for children is that they think that the Government *should* respond to opinion even as they think it doesn't. They see why people protest and know how to. But they do not approve.

'Well I think demonstrating can go a bit far because then violence breaks out and some people can get killed. Well if it's a very small thing

I think they just try to ignore it. If it's quite a big thing and they're getting a lot of complaints . . .'   *(girl, 10)*

Riots are little use, and also destructive. Those taking part in them might get hurt or sent to prison. And yet they feel strongly that some kind of protest should be made. What, then, is the answer to this dilemma?

'Well, we, peaceful rioting . . . peaceful rioting sort of thing. Once the Prime Minister's decided they can't really do anything.'   *(boy, 9)*

The sense of the uselessness of protest rests on the perception of the Prime Minister as immovable. The sense that nothing can be done, that 'it will make no difference' is centred on the idea that 'she just doesn't listen'. Centralized authority is manifested in a collective lack of response:

'You could try by 'phone, unless somebody put a tap on the thing . . . sort of gang up on them. No, they just carry on doing.'   *(boy, 8)*

The only people who do have influence are those who are already in government.

'You can write to the Prime Minister and ask her to change it . . . Well, she'd say, "Oh, it's from a kid. No that can't be very serious".'   *(boy, 10)*

How, after all, can one person make any difference?

'The Prime Minister, a letter, she'll probably think, "OK, I get millions of those a day. I'll ignore that one".'   *(girl, 11)*

Children are aware, again, that it is possible to write, as one way of expressing a point of view. One cites an official reply.

'My friends wrote her a letter. And she sent them a picture of her and she wrote back as well.'   *(girl, 10)*

But action is another thing.

When children balanced their perception of the power of the Prime Minister with a sense of advice received as well as given, they showed themselves aware of the influence of all those in authority, close to the centre of power. They themselves might not be able to make any difference. Crowds of protesters will not prevail. But there are some people who might have the ear of the Premier:

'. . . the big people, you know, with money; yes and landowners.'
(girl, 11)

The 'millions' are not as powerful as the single voice, 'If you got a
job with her' *(girl, 8)*.

'You can't change them unless you're a powerful person. You'd have
to be something big or she wouldn't bother.' *(boy, 9)*

The only real chance children see in making a shift in policy is
through personal persuasion or nepotism. The Prime Minister is
seen as surrounded by a protective wall of guards and relations.

'If she went on a trip, you could go on the trip and tell her about it or
something, but normally there's guards so you can't get out.'
(girl, 10)

'Not unless they know Mrs Thatcher or they were Mrs Thatcher's
brother or sister, would they ever get a chance of stopping it.' *(girl, 9)*

Thus Mrs Thatcher is seen as part of a collective, where the ultimate power lies with her, but there is also influence held by a small
court of people around her: colleagues, friends and relations.

The gap between protest and action remains wide. The most
efficient form of influence is personal persuasion. But the most
successful form of publicity is, of course, television.

'Unless they just go on television and tell everyone, which they have.'
(boy, 10)

Television is there to disseminate points of view. Marches and riots
are set up to appear before the cameras. Children are aware of the
power of the media. For protests to be heard by the public, the
newspapers and television are essential. It is the public form of
communication, just as knowing the Prime Minister is the private
one. Children know that television and newspapers influence the
expression of opinion, rather than the result.

'You could put a headline in a newspaper. They should put things on
the news and ask news reporters to come and see them about things.'
(girl, 9)

'You just get the press and they'll probably get you on television or
something.' *(boy, 10)*

And yet, protest is almost by definition a reaction against something that has already been decided. The sense that there's 'nothing

to be done', that the 'Government's decided' precedes the possibilities of banners, demonstrations and media coverage.

'You could just complain but the Government won't take any notice so that's it.' *(girl, 10)*

The response to any protest can, after all, be through the use of force,

'they'll probably get police in and some of them will probably be arrested' *(boy, 11),*

or through indifference:

'She might just think . . . have a little say up in the Parliament, but then they'll probably just forget it all.' *(girl, 11)*

It might be thought that children's perception of authority in society, embodied in the Government, is one that is formed by the sheer distance between them as individuals and a semi-anonymous bureaucracy based in London. Seeing personalities on television doesn't make them personal. Hearing issues of national importance constantly discussed might not have an immediate local impact. The children were therefore asked about a theoretical local issue, how they felt they could act, and what power they had to influence decisions. The question was whether their general views of politics were applied to an issue of immediate concern. Both children's general perception of the place of the individual in politics and their reflections on a particular case showed the same consistent line. They had little faith in any response to the individual's letter of protest but could think of many ways in which people can protest.

The children were asked about a hypothetical case of a local playground which would be taken over for housing. The question was not so much about the specific playground but about a point of principle; it was chosen because it would affect them all. The children, who naturally felt aggrieved at losing a playground for housing, were also asked what they would think if the houses being built were flats for old people. Just as the children could feel annoyed at losing a playground, so they could feel they could accept losing it for old people. Nevertheless they felt that some kind of compromise could be reached.

But the underlying question was whether children felt that they could protest, and what they would do about it. Their answers again reflected the overall dichotomy between a belief in protest and a lack of belief in its results. The same attitudes that had emerged about national politics were again repeated about local politics. These ranged from the various kinds of demonstrations of opinion that could take place to the indifference with which they felt these demonstrations would be treated. The children were generally quite clear about the distinction between the local council and central government.

> 'The Council only make the rules for this county and the Government makes the rules for the whole country.' *(boy, 11)*

> 'The Government's more important than the Council really.' *(girl, 10)*

> 'The Government tell people where to build things and how to build them usually and the Council usually build the things.' *(boy, 11)*

> 'The Council only have a small bit. The Government has the whole lot.' *(girl, 10)*

Those children who are not clear about the distinction between the spheres of influence rate the importance of the central government to such an extent that they feel its influence is universal. But most children know that there are local politicians as well as national ones, and local as well as national issues, like the building of houses or a playground.

But a local issue does not bring out a different response. The children have little more faith in the power of individual opinion at local level than they do about a national issue.

> 'I don't think I would be able to do anything.' *(girl, 9)*

> 'They'd complain to their Dads and urge their Dads to complain to the council . . . [Do they take any notice?] Notice? No, not really, not with all this stuff going on without it.' *(boy, 9)*

In a local issue, however, one would have thought that there was more chance of gathering together opinions, since there was not the same need for large numbers to protest. Again, the children were willing to contemplate the organization of petitions.

> 'They'd make a petition. Well, different people have different views. They could still want a petition but they might feel that they should have old people's houses.' *(girl, 10)*

The discovery of a decision and the mounting of a protest seem to the children a natural order.

> 'Well, they'd obviously have lots of meetings amongst themselves and try to work out something that can stop the building of it.' *(girl, 10)*

One of two of them have experienced just such a movement:

> 'Well, it was parents who started to moan and that and they sort of called a meeting and things and that and they spoke to people who owned the land.' *(girl, 10)*

One aspect of protest is seen as the organization of opinion so that the sheer number of votes will make a difference. But another side of the protest is envisaged as more of a public demonstration.

> 'They would demonstrate and try to get it changed.' *(girl, 9)*

This isn't considered quite so respectable:

> 'Probably have a march unless if they're that nasty people . . . if they're big strong ones, they might.' *(boy, 10)*

> 'Join a gang and go around cheering and things.' *(boy, 9)*

> 'They would probably protest and be pretty appalled.' *(boy, 10)*

The outer edge of protest is seen as being definite illegal action. The line between illegitimate demonstration and violence or riots is seen as a fine one.

> 'Well, unless they stopped the builders from starting to build the house and knocking everything down, no, I don't think they could do anything.' *(girl, 9)*

Perhaps the children explore the possibilities of such extreme action because they feel that there are no alternatives in making their voice heard. They are still aware of the more normal means of changing opinions, through votes and the collecting of opinions.

> 'They'd ask the committee if they can, if the committee don't agree because they hear all the people complaining and they refuse . . . it doesn't matter what they say. They refuse. They would have to say no. They'd have to have it their way and they'd have to build it somewhere else.' *(girl, 9)*

> 'It depends how many people were actually protesting.' *(boy, 9)*

Again, one or two children had experience of the way in which local opinion could be organized about the council's decision.

> 'They was going to put one up in the Glebe field, then they changed their minds because they have these voting sheets and whoever write "yes" or "no" on the council to put one in, the most votes would either put one in or not have one.' *(boy, 9)*

Although such voting is not pictured as including a system of representations, the sense that children have is that strong feelings can lead to the organization of opinion, and that a general agreement will carry the day. Letters are again seen as the means of presenting their disagreement to the local council, as to central government.

> 'They could write another letter to the Prime Minister.' *(girl, 9)*

> 'Sometimes they do if it's a really big complaint but sometimes they don't take any notice. Writing letters and things and then asking them to build it in another place.' *(boy, 10)*

> 'Write a letter or go to the council offices . . . Well, not from one person but from a lot of people I think they might take more notice.' *(boy, 9)*

> 'Well, they might write a letter to . . . whoever wanted to build homes there, or they might protest about it with all their signs and everything. I hate them.' *(girl, 9)*

The means of legitimate opinion, however, do not automatically lead to any action at local level any more than they do at government level.

> 'Sometimes they can take notice but sometimes they just forget about the point and just break them down sort of thing like that.' *(girl, 10)*

And just as it is assumed to happen with the Prime Minister, knowing the person who makes the decision is considered to be significant.

> 'If I could I would try to kind of, well, say I had a relative kind of that was on the kind of council. I would try to persuade them not to let them . . . if no relative, no good.' *(boy, 9)*

Many of the attitudes on the nature of individual opinion and political decision-making are applied to this particular case. At both national and local level the children view with some scepticism

Children and Society

their ability to effect any change. They consider that the decisions are made by a small number of people who remain indifferent to other people's points of view, unless they are forced to listen to them. Children go on to reflect their belief in the possibility of collective action through petitions, and the organization of demonstrations. At the same time, they are afraid of the overlap between demonstrations and riots, and many of them express some distaste for the paraphernalia of marches, as well as for the excesses, for all the hoardings and banners, as well as the confrontations with the police. These children turn back to the more quiet means of communication, without even mentioning what official channels there are for their opinion to be heard. Given that they see rules made for them from a central source, they assume that any response from even a large number of individuals would be treated with contempt, unless coming from someone who personally knows those in charge. It gives an even clearer picture of a government that is seen to centre on number 10 Downing Street, where 'all' the decisions are made. But then children still show an ambivalent attitude towards making their voice heard; they might not like the fact that they need to use extreme measures when that is the only way, and they do not like demonstrations. But they are aware that demonstrations make the news. The news media, therefore, become a powerful means of spreading opinion, or at least stating it.

'Well, if they said no, I would just . . . move out of the country and get people to say that they would like to put it on television and go to somebody and say, "Can you put this on television?" and say that it's not fair . . .'   *(boy, 9)*

NOTES AND REFERENCES

1. Stradling, R. *The Political Awareness of the School Leaver*. London: Hansard Society, 1977.
2. Connell, R. W. *The Child's Constructional Politics*. Melbourne: University Press, 1971.
3. Cullingford, C. *The Inner World of the School*. London: Cassell, 1991.
4. Lampa, M., and Turiel, E. 'Children's conceptions of adult and peer authority.' *Child Development*, *57*, 405–412, 1986.
5. See Stradling, R., *op. cit.*
6. See Connell, R., *op. cit.*; and Greenstein, F. *Children and Politics*. New Haven: Yale University Press, 1969.

7. Stradling, R., and Zurick, E. 'Political and non-political ideals of English primary and secondary school children.' *Sociological Review*, **19**(2), 203–227, 1971.
8. Hess, R., and Torney, J. *The Development of Political Attitudes in Children.* Chicago: Aldus Publishing Co., 1967.
9. Simmons, C., and Wade, W. 'Young people's least ideals in five countries.' *Educational Review*, **37**(3), 1985.

CHAPTER 5
The Majesty of the Law

'Well, I think if we didn't obey them . . . if we always did obey them, then we wouldn't really need policemen so I think perhaps it's a good thing that some people don't obey them. It provides more jobs.' *(girl, 10)*

The world of government and social control manifests itself in more than one way. On one side stand the politicians, the personalities who wield power, who argue and present themselves as wholly good and rival politicians as bad. Clearly some of the damaging remarks that are made about each other must be true. Politicians are powerful, if frail; they can do good and they can harm. But, on the other side, as a consequence of individual politicians, stands an edifice of rules, agreements collectively made and anonymously imposed. Politicians talk about the way in which they affect lives, for good or ill. But most people are more immediately affected by the laws that govern the country, by restrictions and advice. Children see a connection between the personalities in power and the consequences of their actions, but it is a loose one.

The prime connection between the ideas being promulgated by politicians, and the constraints felt by individuals is the context and the tone in which they take place. Politicians and the law seem concerned with what goes wrong, how to prevent it, how to blame and how to deal with disasters. The context in which social activities are presented in newspapers and on television is one of disasters, natural or man-made. The news, which involves the law from policeman to judges, is concerned with accidents, rapes and disappearances, with murders and explosions. It is then that pictures of all the social forces of the government — ambulances, firemen and policemen — appear. The same forces which have a public and newsworthy role also have local parts to play. The disasters as presented on television might always happen to other people, somewhere else; but the same manifestations of reactions to events are seen close to home. The individual child makes connections between what happens on television and what could happen close to home.

The images that children accumulate of society are of actions and reactions, of people striving to rescue or find each other, to punish or reward. Society is an active series of happenings, rather than an abstract constitution. Just as politicians gain influence by knowing the right person, in what appears to be a secretive way, so courts are seen to be anonymous but controlled by the few. Children seem to take for granted the secretiveness of government, and its lack of close connection with the public at large. The sense that 'nothing can be done' derives from the view of a small number of influential or rich people doing the governing. The same sense pervades the courts. These are run by a coterie of the few, secretly. And yet they are seen to impose rules that affect all.

The constitution is an abstract concept which is rarely discussed. For most individuals it is a concept that only manifests itself in ceremony and ritual: the opening of Parliament by the Queen, and the voice of the Speaker, and only occasionally in an act like voting. It is as if the constitution were separated from the daily business of personal political infighting, and the bear-baiting of the House of Commons. The constitution as such remains hazy not only because it is unwritten but because it is rarely discussed. And yet the peculiar social habits which are manifested in the way a country is governed touch on all lives, in taxes and social security, as well as courts and prisons. There are many habits which are idiosyncratic to one country, and yet they are accepted as if they are as part of some time-honoured and inevitable praxis. Children under 10 are not well informed about the legal system, although they know a lot about the legal vocabulary.[1] They see the manifestations of the law, but are not told how it works. The concepts underlying it remain obscure.

Children's awareness of the law in action, coupled with a lack of explanation of how it works, leads them to create a picture of the law as a series of rules that need to be imposed. Society is therefore hierarchical. The rules are made by the Prime Minister and upheld by the law. The sense of a constitution as a more abstract concept seems to be missing. Instead, the position of government and the actions of society are joined in the imposition of and reaction to, a series of rules, both general and particular. One of the clearest symbols of the law is in the presence of judges and the imposition of sentencing by the courts. The law is understood as the way that society, the governing part of it in particular, imposes its will in constraining an otherwise ungovernable population.

There is, therefore, a tension between an abstract constitution and pragmatic laws. Children, after all, understand rules, and the need for rules, from their own experience. But some things remain obscure. The Prime Minister is seen by children as being ultimately responsible for decisions that affect people. But the way in which these decisions are made part of the constitution remains obscure. The political realities of the House of Commons, and voting for the enactment of the law through political parties, is not as clearly manifested as television pictures of the Prime Minister talking, travelling and opening new buildings. Something as complex as the raising of revenue does not have a clear definition in children's minds. But the law is a different matter. Children are all aware of rules, of certain codes, and of the social decisions they must follow. Just as in school the hierarchical nature of the system manifests itself in a series of rules to be followed, so does the expression of central government. Children in school think that rules are extremely important, and actually assume that they become more important as people become older, since the older people are the more they are inclined to depravity.

The law is a significant feature in children's idea of the State. But their attitudes towards the law are far more equivocal than one might have thought likely. They do not automatically associate law and morality. They recognize that the law is constantly broken. In school they see rules as sanctions imposed on them rather than agreed social necessities. The idea that the law is there to guide how people should behave is almost never mentioned. Instead, the law must be obeyed because you would be punished if you didn't. The law, therefore, is an instrument of power, administered by the police and by a system of punishments. The law consists of:

> 'Commandments. Don't drink and drive. You're not allowed to kill each other.' *(girl, 9)*

The morality of not killing others might be so obvious as to make pointing it out unnecessary. But one of the reasons for the way in which children view the law is its association with particular rules that have little to do with morality as such. Virtually all the children stated that the law was to do, primarily, with speed limits or driving on the left-hand side of the road, which are decisions reached on pragmatic grounds. Even the other laws that children mentioned most often, like drinking and driving and wearing seat belts, have a pragmatic dimension in attempting to limit the damage done to people. It was only when children were pressed to remember more laws that they recalled the more general social ones like sanctions against rape and murder. For children, and for most adults, the law is theoretical until it comes to driving a car, or to other domestic rules, like not drinking under age. There has been nothing as important as private transport or, possibly, drugs in bringing the possibility of breaking the law close to people's everyday lives. Children see laws are there to prevent you doing certain things. 'Thou shalt not' is the general sanction. And the most immediate of rules is not to drive without a seat belt and not to drink and drive. Whilst not affecting these children personally, they are most aware of those laws which have been constantly advertised.

The law is a system of rules at a variety of levels. Most people are affected by the immediate ones. The laws of which children are most immediately aware are those which are domestic, especially those which are concerned with 'rules' of the road. Some are a matter of convention, like not going the wrong way down one-way streets. The first rules that children bring to mind are to do with traffic regulations

> 'Not to go over seventy miles an hour.' *(girl, 7)*

> 'You're not allowed to drive a car until you're 17.' *(girl, 8)*

> 'Well, I don't know many laws. Don't get married until you're 18, don't ride a motor cycle until you're 16, don't drive a car until you're 18.' *(boy, 9)*

> 'Not allowed to drink and then drive, not allowed to go over seventy, not allowed to drive on the opposite side of the road.' *(boy, 10)*

There are very few exceptions to the prevailing attitude that the most visible and immediate aspect of the law is the code of driving. There are, after all, immediate sanctions if the law is not obeyed, and it is the aspect of the law most likely to be broken. The law is associated with *rules*, as if the rules of behaviour in school were translated into a more public sphere. The law therefore is not associated with morality, nor with justice, but with regulations that need to be enforced. It is as if social order was a matter of convention, and as if these conventions in the public sphere, on the roads, were there for the police to control.

> 'The laws are like . . . in cars there's a limit. There's a law . . . if you go over the law, the limit, you're breaking the law.' *(boy, 9)*

This is the pragmatic way in which the law is defined.

The law, as a series of regulations, is seen to apply to domestic circumstances in the first instance. Children's first thought is of what they, or their parents, are not allowed to do.

> 'Not drink too much. Not to, really, kind of take drugs and that. Not to go really fast on the roads.' *(boy, 9)*

Those children who live in rural areas add their particular awareness of the rules of the countryside to the rules of the road:

> 'Um . . . driving at certain speeds, wearing a seat belt. I think there's going to be a law for wearing a riding hat.' *(girl, 9)*

> 'Poaching, I think. When they go and kill birds and rabbits without it being allowed . . . Don't drink and drive over the limit, don't speed over the limit . . .' *(girl, 10)*

In place of the mystery that might surround the law, with arcane procedures, and unusual costumes, children see laws are affecting them in a practical way. The law is not the manifestation of a code of justice, creating guilt or fear, nor a system of directly applied morality, but, essentially, regulations that are imposed by the State. There might be moral reasons for these rules, but the children see the rules as statements, meant to be obeyed.

> 'Not to bring dogs in, that have got diseases.' *(girl, 10)*

> 'Um, about seat belts, then, well, one of them is, I think you have to wear a special hat. I mean there are still people who go out with no hat on at all.' *(girl, 10)*

The law is not so much to do with patterns of behaviour; it does not strike children as starting from a moral code. Their first line of reasoning was that the law is essentially to do with regulations.

'It's non-smoking day today. That's one of the rules. Drunken drivers?
. . . Selling false tapes, computer tapes and that . . .'   *(boy, 9)*

Children think of the law at two levels. Their first reactions are to
do with immediate rules that should be kept. Only when pressed to
think of any other laws do children go beyond the domestic into the
more serious aspects of the law, concerned with violent behaviour.
Children are conscious of immediate rules and regulations which
affect them or their families, rather than the more general concern
about burglary, or hurting people. Nevertheless they are all aware
of the importance of the police in maintaining some order, or in
punishing those people who are violent. Children might see rules
affecting cars but are all made aware, through the news, of the
everyday existence of killing, rape and murder. The second level of
the law is also then manifested.

'Don't kill people and you can't smuggle drugs. You can't break into
anything or steal anything.'   *(girl, 8)*

'Not allowed to . . . um . . . kill anybody or anything.'   *(girl, 9)*

'Stealing and murdering and smuggling and drugs.'   *(girl, 11)*

'Stealing, killing.'   *(boy, 8)*

'You mustn't shoot a policeman. You mustn't rob or burgle someone.'
(girl, 8)

'Um, stealing. What to do and what not to do. You must not steal,
write on walls, injure people and shoot them with guns, rob banks.'
(boy, 10)

Children find it difficult to make the distinction between levels of
crime. All are rules, whether against litter or against killing and all
earning sanctions if they are disobeyed:

'Not throwing litter around and not spitting, things like that, murdering and things.'   *(boy, 10)*

Whilst most of the children put domestic rules first, and then
add more serious crimes, all revealed that to them the law is a mixture of things that regulates not just extreme behaviour but more
routine matters. Children felt they needed to be aware of the law
in case they would break it. The law is associated with many things
that they are *not* supposed to do. Laws are, to that extent, negative, a question of sanctions rather than any positive moral

commandments about how to behave. The sense of compulsion affects all levels of the law.

> 'You have to wear a safety belt. It's compulsory. You're not allowed drinking and driving. Drugs. All things like that.' *(girl, 11)*

Children know that some crimes are more important than others, but still show into how many levels the law spreads, until a whole mixture of regulations is called to mind:

> 'Murder . . . Manslaughter. And that's not quite as bad. Half as bad. You have to pay a certain amount at least. You're not allowed to keep things which are in your own garden. Treasures, for instance . . . you have to go by the one-way sign if there is one. And you're not allowed to go the wrong way on the wrong side of the road.' *(girl, 9)*

To children the law works at all levels, without discrimination. It is an edifice of practical rules, a series of 'don'ts'.

> 'Not murdering children . . . Not to drive too fast. Not to burgle other people.' *(girl, 8)*

> 'We mustn't drink and drive. Mustn't speed. Mustn't do careless driving. Well you're not allowed to use guns in this country. You're not meant to kill anybody, otherwise you'd go to gaol.' *(girl, 10)*

> 'The seat-belt law and double yellow lines for parking. It's against the law to murder and steal.' *(girl, 10)*

> 'There's rules against crime, such as burglary, smuggling and murder. Laws against licensing, taxes . . .' *(boy, 11)*

> 'Wear a seat belt in cars. Not use lead weights when you're fishing. Drive on the right side of the road. Keep a certain speed. Well, we're not meant to murder each other.' *(boy, 11)*

One of the main reasons that children are aware of the many levels of the law is that they are aware of the sanctions that prevent people from breaking the law. The essential reason for the law in children's eyes is that without it, there would be chaos. It is there to control people's natural tendencies to do what they want to do.

> 'There's lots of driving laws. There are lots of people making riots and being cruel to animals and children.' *(girl, 9)*

> 'Driving on the left-hand side of the road . . . drinking under age. You're not allowed to drink under 18 and you have to go to school as well . . . fighting, murdering, that sort of thing. It helps

because there are some mad people that go around killing each other.'
(girl, 10)

'A lot of them, people don't obey at all, like driving with your seat belt
on.' *(boy, 10)*

The problem with seeing the law as a list of regulations is that
children become aware of how easily laws can be broken. There is
no aura of morality and guilt when some rules are so everyday that
people are seen to break them constantly. At the same time children
hear of and see pictures of all those people who have broken more
serious laws: murder, arson, theft and abductions are the ways in
which the law is highlighted. Given that the law is seen to regulate
many levels of behaviour, children are aware of the importance of
how the law is managed. Part of their pragmatism is the realization
that the law depends on enforcement, on catching criminals, in
making sure that people do not drink and drive. Such rules create in
children a sense of an almost mechanical structure, of regulations
and punishments.

Sometimes the regulations appear to have an immediate connection to everyday behaviour:

'Stop rioting. Don't push people in water. Don't park in public places.
Don't throw stones at other people.' *(boy, 10)*

Just as children are aware that school rules are constantly broken,
so they know that the law is broken. They assume that regulations
are necessary, given natural human depravity, and they see that
the real power of the law depends not just on enforcement but on
punishment. It is not only 'mad' people or 'rioters' who break laws,
but people who drive cars.

'You have to put your seat belt on when you're in a car, which my Dad
doesn't do. He just forgets. He just puts it on and I say, "Daddy, do it
up," and he says "Pardon," and turns the radio up in the car so that he
can't hear me.' *(boy, 10)*

Children are made aware that rules are broken, not only at home
and in school but throughout society as a whole. They cite examples
of school rules and how they are broken:

'You're not really allowed to ride on the pavement . . . but people do,
in this school.' *(boy, 8)*

And they are reminded on the news about those people who break the laws:

> 'I don't know any laws. About stop thiefs. Some people do still shoot, though, don't they? I think they're mad!' *(girl, 10)*

Children assume that all laws are broken. Perhaps it is this belief that gives so little moral edge to their views. The sense of ultimate justice is as distant from their views as it is from the law itself.

> '. . . everybody breaks laws so it's hard to think of some. If you're really strict, like no burglaries, everybody's going to break that because they think it's silly.' *(girl, 11)*

Laws are there to control society. When they are inevitably broken there is a need to find and punish the criminal. There is little sense that the laws are dependent on a view of human behaviour. The law is not considered a moral force, but a necessary counterpart to human depravity. There is therefore little sense of awe for the imposed rules. Not only do many people clearly break the law, but many people are heard speaking out against some of the laws. Whilst children accept their necessity they do not think of the law as a universally shared belief.

> 'Well, some are all right and some aren't . . . well, smoking and seat belts . . . it won't change.' *(girl, 8)*

Even if the law will not change, there are many details that many do not agree with. Some children point out that people generally cannot be bothered and there will always be those with criminal tendencies — like football hooligans. Criminals are always with us. But then children find it easy to disagree with the laws.

> 'Well, some are good but some are really stupid. Because, for instance, there's films that you can't see if you are certain age and I was quite lucky to see the *Thriller* video because it was a so-called "X". But some of them I agree that they should be unsuitable for young children, but some of them there's no point.' *(girl, 9)*

There is always a hint that private actions should be outside, or beyond the law.

> 'Drinking driving . . . um . . . vandalism . . . Have a fight and it's not like wrestling in a thing . . . it's just between two people.' *(boy, 10)*

The law is viewed as an edifice of prevention and punishment. None of the children speaks in terms of ethics. To them the structure of the law is a pragmatic one, in which laws apply at different levels to different people. The law consists of sanctions on behaviour, including behaviour which cannot easily be seen to contain a moral dimension. The question in their minds is, therefore, whether the law should always be obeyed and if so, why? Nearly all the children agreed that the law should be obeyed, usually. But they were also equivocal about the reasons, and could think of exceptions. They also suggest that some of the laws are somewhat equivocal. There is no sense of their seeing the law as a perfect structure, of a series of commandments that have to be obeyed for reasons of scruple. They would agree that laws needed to be obeyed.

'Yes . . . as much as you can.' *(girl, 9)*

'Well, you should really obey it.' *(boy, 9)*

But already there is an equivocal note. They suggest that the law should be obeyed because it is there, and you would be punished if you did not.

'It's the law and you just have to put up with it.' *(boy, 8)*

'Yes, I'd still obey it but I wouldn't really like it that much.' *(girl, 10)*

Children know that in the variety of manifestations of the law there are bound to be some marginal laws with which they disagree. The wider the sense of rules and regulations, the less respect there is for the idea of law. They witness their parents' antipathy to some regulations, like having to wear seat belts:

'They explain to the police that they don't want to wear one. They just have to because it's the law.' *(boy, 11)*

They also witness the anguish which the law can cause.

'Because there's this man in our lane called Mr H., and he thinks he owns all the land but Daddy does, so Daddy thinks it's unfair. Well, at night he plays with his computer and when he gets bored of it he sits down and starts muttering things about Mr H.' *(girl, 7)*

But the general feeling is that everyone has to put up with the law whether they like it or not.

'Just try to stick with it and try to overcome that you don't like it.' *(boy, 11)*

'It's a bit of tough luck isn't it?' *(girl, 10)*

They often suggest that they do not always want to obey all rules. They *must* obey the law. They do not feel that they necessarily *ought* to, not in every instance.

'Well, you haven't got to if you don't want to.' *(boy, 9)*

There is little impression of respect for the law. Once it is manifested in the regulation of private lives as well as public behaviour, there is a tendency to take it less seriously. Many children find aspects of the law silly or unfair. They not only see how often they can get away from obeying rules, but see parents and others equivocate with speed limits or seat belts. And they also observe how many people, in their own country and elsewhere, perpetrate unlawful acts. They know that people do not obey the law. They see numerous films and series on television describing in detail ways of doing wrong, thereby triggering the association of law with the police and retribution. They know that the law is not obeyed partly because of people's tendency towards bad behaviour, and partly because the law is not vigorously enough enforced. But they also criticize the limitations of the law in some of its details.

'Yes, but I think some of them are a bit silly . . . Well, you should [obey] but a lot of people don't.' *(boy, 10)*

'Sometimes I think the laws are a bit silly, but most of the time I approve of them. Yes, you've got to obey them whether they're right or wrong, in any sense.' *(boy, 10)*

This distinction between the necessity to obey the law, and the view that the law is not always correct, is a central one in the minds of children.

'I think we should obey them, but some of them are pretty silly. Yes, not allowing children into pubs. It's not as though they're going to drink.' *(boy, 9)*

But they also feel that there is little that they can do about it.

'There are a few that are a bit dodgy . . . you can't change them unless you're a powerful person.' *(boy, 9)*

When some laws seem to make sense it still does not change the assumption that the rules are often arbitrary, as in the case of licensing laws or the rules of the road. Laws are looked at pragmatically.

> 'Some of them, like safety belts, because that saved my mother but some of the things are a bit stupid . . . you can't do much really.' *(girl, 11)*

The problem with elaborate rules lies not just in disagreeing with some of them but in interpreting them. The licensing laws that support the assumption of some publicans that underage children would drink alcohol is a case in point. The question of whether the spreed limit is fixed at absolutely the right level for all circumstances is another. And then there is the question of the private and the public. Should people (of either sex) be allowed to do things that do not offend others, like driving faster than the speed limit?

> 'Oh, well, I wouldn't think that was fair. I'd most probably go on to the tracks where you are allowed to go fast. If I was a man, anyway, I'd do that. If I was a woman I'd just obey the strict orders.' *(girl, 10)*

Children obey the law because they have to, but note that there can be good reasons as well as bad ones for ignoring the law. The threat of sanctions balances the sense of personal licence in following their own desires.

Children can give examples of circumstances when there are reasons for not strictly obeying the law.

> 'Not on some things . . . like, say, if you was going too fast in the car, but it might be a rush to get somewhere, like if somebody's injured.' *(boy, 9)*

Some children suggest that they wouldn't obey, even without such an explicit reason, as in the wearing of seat belts:

> 'I wouldn't wear one.' *(boy, 11)*

Even those who say that one ought to obey, can add:

> 'I just wouldn't obey it.' *(girl, 9)*

as if there were not strong moral sanctions being imposed, as if they would 'ignore it' unless they had the 'bad luck' to be caught by the police. Sometimes children's sense of the control of the law comes across as if such rules were nothing but a constant imposition.

> 'Well, they're sort of ruling our lives. When we have a sort of free country, we could do what we like as long as we don't get drunk and drive unsteady. Laws . . . too bossy. I think we should have a free country.' *(boy, 8)*

It should be added that the same boy assumes that such freedom would lead to an increase in the incidence of rape. The sense of personal freedom can come across in a very different form, as when a girl protests against the law in the following terms:

> 'I would say, "No thank you, I'd better not, it's not very good to do that."' *(girl, 7)*

Children make a distinction between the need to obey the law, and their belief in it. They are also aware of different aspects of the law: on the one hand, laws aimed against immoral behaviour, and on the other, laws which are the result of agreed patterns of behaviour. Their equivocations about the law depend on what kind of law it is. The law is never found to be wholly silly or unfair.

> 'Well, in some terms, but some laws are so silly you can't always obey them . . . it depends on what law it is really.' *(boy, 10)*

> 'It depends really what it's about. If it's something to do with speed limits, they could change it. But they might not, though.' *(girl, 10)*

The essential distinction is between the laws that are central and those which are more arbitrary.

> 'Well, if it's something like the limits . . . sort of, if you thought that, um . . . seventy was sort of not very fast and you sort of don't agree, you go over it but if it's sort of very important, like stealing, you do.' *(girl, 11)*

> 'I reckon we should [obey] about the kidnapping and the murdering but some of them . . . well . . .' *(girl, 11)*

There are, of course, visible on the news, many people who are constantly protesting against the law. This throws a particular light on obedience to the law, as when it appears that protesters have a clear cause:

> 'It depends really. Some people, they don't like the law. Like the peace women.' *(boy, 10)*

Children do not think of the law as sacrosanct. They are able to disagree with some rules, thereby showing how pragmatic and piecemeal is their view of it. There might be a highly organized *system* but this has more to do with enforcement than with a social or moral code to which they are committed. They feel that they ought to obey but also feel that there could well be aspects of the law with which they would disagree. Instead of an optimistic view of society, in which all laws work together for good, children express an equivocal attitude:

> 'You should try to obey really, but if you don't really like it I don't know what you would do.' *(girl, 10)*

The feeling that the law has been built up on firm principles or a general consensus in never conveyed. They associate politicians, after all, with creating rules. As regulations are supposed to stem from personalities, so the choice of whether to 'put up with them' or not becomes a personal issue.

> 'If you're the sort of kind of person that you've obeyed every other rule then you sort of stop and you hesitate and . . .' *(girl, 10)*

And just as nothing can be done to change the mind of the Prime Minister, so nothing can be done about aspects of the law that seem unjust.

> 'They can't really do anything. Complain? Not really. Well, they could but it wouldn't do any good.' *(boy, 10)*

Whilst children question aspects of law, and hold on to their right to question, and even disobey, they are stringent about other people who break the law. They have little sympathy for rioters and football hooligans. This kind of double standard comes about not only because it is common to feel the distinction between personal behaviour and other people, but because of the difference between violence and petty infringements. It derives from the sense that the law is supported by fear of punishment, that all the forces of order, the courts and the police, are there to make sure that the law is enforced.

The reason for submitting to law is that if you didn't you would be punished. The balance of the invocations of 'don'ts' — don't steal, don't flash your lights, don't murder people, don't break the speed limit — are the consequences if you do.

'You're not meant to kill anybody. Otherwise you'd go to gaol.' *(girl, 10)*

'. . . or else you'll go to prison for about one or two years.'   *(boy, 10)*

The reasons for obedience are clear:

'Sometimes it's not fair, but obey 'cos otherwise you'll be into even more trouble.'   *(boy, 11)*

Children have mixed feelings about whether these punishments act as deterrents or merely as inevitable consequences of behaviour. They also wonder whether punishments lead to reform. On the whole they take the threat of punishment seriously at a personal level but doubt whether others do.

'Well, you might obey it, but if you get caught then you have a fine and you'll probably obey it eventually.'   *(boy, 11)*

The personal sense of guilt is not as strong as the fear of retribution:

'Well, I wouldn't want to get told off by the police. My Dad never wears his seat belt.'   *(girl, 9)*

As children get older so their ideas of the need for punishment become stronger.[2] But this does not mean that harsher punishments mean a more moral position; on the contrary, they also become more lenient in terms of moral judgements. Nevertheless they feel that the standard form of social punishment, prison, is a necessity, a natural consequence of robbery. Rules are there to be enforced: prison is both punishment and the prevention of a repetition, at least for a time. Thus prisons are seen as a central part of the machinery of the law; the law would have no meaning if there were no punishment. Prison is seen as the equivalent of detention in school, a consequence of action, but not always a cure.

'Maybe put them in prison for a while or something to teach them.'   *(girl, 9)*

'But people still do it, and they get put in prison for doing that.'   *(boy, 9)*

Children have mixed views about whether prisons are designed to reform their inmates or merely to incarcerate them for a time. The essential fact of prison as punishment is accepted in itself; prisons are part of the system, for whatever reasons. Going to prison can be likened to going to a 'mental health camp'. People need to learn through punishment.

> 'Prison if it's an older person, and then it's a punishment and so you probably won't do it again.' *(boy, 10)*

> 'The police put them into prison if they're very, very bad and do lots of bad things.' *(girl, 8)*

Children see prison as the appropriate consequence of crime. They seem to approve of prison as a necessary support to the law.

> 'They should be put in prison. They should be stopped and checked.' *(boy, 9)*

> 'I think they should put some of them in prison.' *(girl, 8)*

There are clear actions that people 'ought' to take, to prevent any crime:

> 'They get put in gaol, so they can't get out and do it again.' *(girl, 8)*

Children are familiar with sentencing, with the differences between the amounts of time, including life, that prisoners receive. They do not seem, however, to be aware of the parole system. But then a number imply that they would wish to see harsher punishments. If criminals do not change their habits, runs the argument, they need to be put away for longer. There is no sense of the possibility of reform.

> 'They do horrible things and they go in gaol for their time but when they come out, about a week later, they plan something and just come back and do it again.' *(boy, 10)*

That sense that the system does not work well is conveyed not only through the remarks about lenient sentences but a realization that criminals are not always caught:

> 'You get put in gaol. That's if you ever get caught.' *(girl, 9)*

Whilst nearly all the children recommend harsher punishments and more successful enforcement, there are some who do not understand exactly how the legal system and the prison system work. This can cause, for a few, some worries about the appropriateness of punishments to the crime, if prison sentences appear to be a response to all offences.

'I don't agree with the rules sometimes. Locking someone in a cage if they do something to another person . . . it's like a cage. I don't mind about the very bad ones, like killing someone, but if you just are naughty about the roads or something I don't think they would be put in prison. Not for long anyway.' *(boy, 8)*

The idea of prison is so central for children that, although they are aware of other punishments, like fines, it becomes almost symbolic of society's desire to control unruly elements. After all, with two exceptions, the children knew of no worse punishment than prison, and of the two who mentioned hanging, one only applied it to the most serious of all possible offences.

'You can still be hanged, you can, if you destroy some of the Prime Minister's things.' *(boy, 10)*

Children's references to prisons show how they understand the workings of the legal system. They understand the mechanics of the processes without concern for the reasons behind them. Their insight into the working out of the law is pragmatic. They might not agree with all the rules, and be able to cite some laws they do not agree with, but they see the inevitable processes of being caught and punished as part of the working out of legal cause and effect. The law is enforced by its officers:

'Laws are groups of people . . . the police.' *(boy, 9)*

The first stage in the process of law is to catch criminals:

'They've hardly got no money and they take your jewels. A policeman goes after them and catches them.' *(girl, 8)*

The prisoner, being caught, gets taken away,

'They take us away to places . . . sometimes courts, sometimes stations to talk.' *(boy, 10)*

The relationship, then, between gaol and court is a close one:

'They can go to court; be put in gaol sometimes.' *(boy, 7)*

But children are aware that courts can give a variety of different sentences, even if incarceration is central.

'You go to court and afterwards you might go to prison. You get fined.' *(girl, 10)*

'Put you in gaol. Keep you there until you own up. They take you to court.' *(boy, 10)*

It is at the court that crucial decisions are made. The wrongdoers having been caught, the sentencing then takes place.

'You go to court. And the judge decides whether you should be kept in prison or be left free.' *(girl, 11)*

The sense that people are in prison immediately after being arrested testifies to the strength of the impression made by the penal code. Prisons are on the news; the desire to catch criminals and put them away is the motive of police drama. Although children know about bail and understand fines, the court's role is seen as essentially one of sentencing the guilty to terms in prison. The court's role in the system of punishment is to judge not whether someone is innocent or guilty, but whether they should go to gaol, and for how long. This implies more of a pragmatic acceptance of courts rather than a sense of a perfect moral system:

'You go to court and they might be very lenient, might be pretty heavy, but usually you come out of it.' *(girl, 11)*

There is a sense of human judgements, even idiosyncratic decisions behind the sentences of the court.

To some children, however, the court is not just part of the system of punishment and regulation but a place where arguments about possible wrongs can take place. One of the few alternatives to unofficial protest, like demonstrations, is to co-ordinate the feeling of many people through official channels. For just two children the legal system is a possible alternative to pickets, or private influence:

'Well, you can go against the court, sometimes . . . I think you go to court and ask for the reasons and things like that . . . It's not quite easy. It is sometimes but some of the things can be rather hard.' *(girl, 10)*

'You could go to court about it or something.' *(boy, 11)*

But the legal system is not generally associated with putting things right, or with arguing for justice.

Children view the legal system in a fairly mechanistic way. When we unravel all the evidence that they give it is clear that there are certain aspects of the law that are particularly salient. Given the propensity for individuals to break the rules, the legal system is seen as a means of controlling, catching and punishing criminals. If we remind ourselves of the presentation of courts and criminals on television we must note that there are certain actions, like sentencing and imprisoning, that stand out vividly. The first impressions of the law are derived second-hand, as a series of dramas, rather than experienced personally or explained. Jurisprudence is a subject seen to be fitted to a university syllabus; the constitutional aspects of the law are rarely tackled by those outside the legal system. It is not surprising, then, that children see the law in terms of a series of rules, at a variety of levels. They do not present any idea of the law as sacrosanct, at the service of justice, or to protect the individual. The law is punishment.

The aspects of the law that children cite and those which ring in their minds are a mixture of the theatrical, the moral and the everyday:

'You're not allowed to steal and everything like that. You're not allowed to go on other people's property. Trespass. You're not allowed to . . . I've forgotten . . . to go into places unless you pay for them and . . . you're not allowed to take shotguns into the town and go into the town unless you've got a licence.' *(boy, 10)*

But the main injunction is in the phrase, 'You're not allowed to'. The law is there to stop people doing certain things, whether they agree with the law or not. Children therefore are not brought up to have deeply held respect for the law. Those involved in the law might have a strong sense of its majesty but it is not shared by the younger generation. The law is seen as the imposition of rules, the regulation of punishment and the framework for the police.

NOTES AND REFERENCES

1. Flin, R., Stevenson, Y., and Davies, G. 'Children's knowledge of court proceedings.' *British Journal of Psychology* **80**(3), 285–297, 1989.
2. Farnham, A., and Jones, S. 'Children's views regarding possessions and their theft.' *Journal of Moral Education* **16**(1), 18–30, 1987.

CHAPTER 6

The Strong Arm of the Law: The Police

'They're sort of like the other side of the riot people. The good side. They have those sort of big sort of shields.' *(girl, 9)*

The law depends on enforcement. Children's views of the State, the courts and the prevention of crime are strongly influenced by their attitudes to the police. The police are there to make sure that the law is obeyed, that criminals are captured and that people are told off when they are breaking the rules. They are involved not only with significant crimes but in enforcing the rules of the road. The picture that children have of the police is complex but very clear. The ways in which the police are presented on the news is made apparent by the ways in which children describe them. Children accept the fundamental need for a police force, but do not have any romantic notions of their behaviour.

There is a general assumption that the police need to present a good image of themselves to the community. Many police forces make a point of visiting schools to further knowledge of how they work and to gain co-operation from the community.[1] Indeed, they see a connection between discipline in schools and behaviour in society.[2] But, as this chapter makes clear, children have a rather bleaker view of the police than the latter might like. They associate the police with a variety of images that contrast sharply with the notion of the friendly local constable. This is not to say that children consider the police as unhelpful. They know that the police do their best:

'Well, the police are good people. They try to help old people when things have gone wrong.' *(boy, 9)*

But children consider that the police are so involved in difficult circumstances that they are bound to be compromised by them.

Children are aware of the complexities of a policeman's role and the fact that each is part of a large organization. Policemen are, after all, often seen in massed ranks as well as on the street.

81

'The police just do what they're told. If there's lots of policemen they just get told what to do, but if it's just the policeman on the beat, he does what he thinks is best.' *(boy, 9)*

The police are also envisaged as having decisions to make, as well as fulfilling orders. They are so much a part of law that there are occasional hints that children see them as able to change it.

'Try to talk to the police to see if they can sort of make it into a different rule.' *(girl, 9)*

But the everyday decisions that the police have to make are to do with how they react to events.

'They have to keep an eye on you and if they see you're doing something wrong, they stop you and they write your name and things down and then they can fine you.' *(girl, 10)*

The reactive role of the police includes keeping a watchful eye on what goes on, with a view of stepping in when there is a crime or an accident. They are involved with the public on the scenes of car crashes and, more rarely, with criminal cases:

'If somebody shoots somebody they have to go and see the person who saw and then they have a description of the person and they can look for them.' *(girl, 10)*

The sense of the individual policeman does not figure as strongly as the more general idea of a police force as a whole. This is not just to do with the rarity of seeing an officer 'on the beat' — 'You don't often see police walking about as there's a police station there.' (girl, 9) — but because of the more spectacular presentations of police activities when they are involved in riots or serious crime. The role of the police can seem almost anonymous in its complexity. Behind the massed ranks there is a large bureaucracy.

'People get in touch with them and say what's happened and they have to trace . . . search to see if they've had any previous record and things . . .' *(girl, 10)*

The role of the police might be seen in anonymous terms but the impact of what they do does not lie as much in the detective work but in more obvious action. The same girl, describing the role of the police, continues:

'. . . they've been shooting . . . the plastic bullets. They're all right to fire into the air or something, but they have actually missed and shot people . . . they have barriers and shields and things.'

The co-ordination of police activity of which children are most conscious is centred around confrontations:

'Try to stop them and go to the place where they're having riots with their shields, get more equipment in and just try and stop people from doing all the things.' *(girl, 11)*

The impression that is given by the police is distinctly physical — anonymous and physical.

The organization of the police, supported by equipment, to 'inspect crimes', is acknowledged as a bureaucracy in support of the law. But just as children's ideas of the legal system focus on courts, prisons and punishments, so their sense of the police as servants of that system focuses on the most physical aspects of crime prevention. They not only catch criminals but 'hold people apart'. And just as there are hints of the arbitrariness of the law, so there is a distinct impression in children's minds that the police are capable of making the wrong decisions.

'Sometimes they mistake people and put them in gaol and they're the wrong people. They just take them because somebody's just hit somebody and I hit a lot of people at my school and I don't get put into gaol.' *(boy, 10)*

It might be thought that with so many television series that extol the ultimate infallibility of the police, there could be a romantic aura to detective work, with a sense of justice at the core. But real policemen do not have this image. It is as if children instinctively know about (although they do not mention) low detection rates for crime. They also sense how easy it is for the police to make mistakes against innocent people. This is not an impression which suggests the occasional lapse but one which permeates all police activity. The police need to arrest people, but often this is 'not fair'.

'Sometimes I think they are a bit too tough on some people. Sort of they capture . . . they get some people who sort of haven't really done too much and then there are other people who've done things which are much worse and they're just leaving them free.' *(girl, 9)*

The reason for this sense of possible injustice is that the police are given the means to make mistakes. Children see the police having to make quick, sometimes violent, decisions. They are armed with weapons such as plastic bullets that can harm people. They wield truncheons and carry riot shields. If there is no other way of controlling people except by force, there are bound to be mistakes.

'Sometimes they do things wrong, like fire plastic bullets at people. That can kill them if it hits them in the heart or something, but most of the time they're just protecting themselves with riot shields. When a riot's in full swing they hit people with truncheons but what they've done to the police, there sometimes is no other way of controlling people except by force.' *(boy, 10)*

Given the means to make mistakes, children accept that accidents will happen. They remember incidents that they have seen on the news.

'I heard on the news that a policeman shot a lady by accident.' *(boy, 10)*

'One policeman shot a 5-year-old boy.' *(girl, 11)*

The news is an important source for children's knowledge of the police, partly because of the general imagery of policing, and partly because of the stories that they hear. The police have gained a reputation for making mistakes and having prejudices. Certain incidents seem to become part of the mythology of the police.

'I think, like, at that Bradford fire, one of the supporters could have put it out just by stamping on it, but the police wanted him to stay back. That's what started it. There was a small flame. He was going to put it out and a policeman told him to get back.' *(boy, 9)*

News consists of what is most sensational and most disturbing. Stories about the police centre on all the aspects of police decisions that have gone wrong, either shooting people or corruption.

'I think I heard on the news once . . . one policeman, when they shot people not about the legs, waist — things like that. I heard that some break the laws themselves, like that one that drank. In a way they make things worse a bit. I think they have too many at one place.' *(girl, 9)*

Certain incidents stand out, like a shooting. But the sense of police fallibility is a more pervasive, more general one. Individual incidents are given as examples of a more general theme.

'It shows on the news them training and all that, but it said sometimes they all go wild and that.' *(boy, 10)*

The police also have a general reputation for racial prejudice. Having acquired it, there are a number of particular examples that demonstrate this. Just as an audience will remember those things that fit in with their prejudices, and just as they will listen to politicians that they agree with, so children accumulate stories that support a general impression.[3]

'On the news last night there was this lady who was complaining that just because her husband was black and her baby was brown there were threats to kill the baby and she said the police weren't doing anything about it, even though she had written a letter to them. The police are ignoring some letters and doing a lot to other letters. It's just that sometimes they seem to ignore them.' *(girl, 9)*

'I've heard it on the news. One policeman shot somebody. Beating up black people, because they don't like the black people very much. They were questioning a white person and he had some black friends with him and he just sort of said, ''Go away Blackie''.' *(boy, 9)* .

It is very hard to expunge the effect of single incidents if the audience see each one as typical and as fitting into a more general pattern. The attitudes towards ethnic minorities are examples of the mistakes the police make — from shooting people to favouring some over others.

Children are very conscious of the negative aspects of the police, as well as of their necessity. This reaction is not just an abstract one. The incidents they cite do not only happen in some other part of the country. Children's prejudices enter into their personal knowledge of the police.

'They annoy people. They're everywhere. If you're just sitting in the street talking to someone, like an old lady or someone, they just come up to you and say, ''you're nicked,'' and take you away.' *(boy, 10)*

The sense of personal threat, however, is not as pervasive as the sense that if there is any local problem the police won't do anything about it.

'I think we asked them about the [dumped] car a couple of weeks ago but they haven't done anything about it.' *(girl, 9)*

This reaction to the police, seeing them as too busy tackling violent crime to care about domestic difficulties, is held despite a widely expressed desire to like the police. Children are not wholly negative. But they all share an insight into the police force that assumes that there will be mistakes, that corruption takes place and that the police have almost become part of the world of violence that they seek to control. The police are seen as having a difficult, unpleasant and unrewarding job.

> 'I used to want to be a policeman, but I don't think I do at the moment. Because of everything they have to do . . . .' *(boy, 9)*

In the general debates about law and order there is a dichotomy about the role of the police force. On the one hand is the need for community policing, for the 'bobby on the beat', for close and friendly relationships with the neighbourhood and the policeman as a friend. On the other hand, the police need to control crime, to catch criminals, to bring people to justice. For anyone who drives a car, the policeman is a potential enemy — the law-enforcer rather than friend. Perhaps there is bound to be a tension between these two points of view. It is clear that such an ambiguity about the policeman's role affects children. On the one hand, children find the police helpful and well-meaning. On the other, they see them in conditions of violence, in which they are not assumed to be innocent.

The image of the police force that children hold in their minds is not of the individual constable, but of massed ranks trying to keep order in a riot. This vision is not only a result of the vivid scenes presented on television news, but is a natural outcome of the idea of a large organization embroiled in the battle against crime, rather than an organization at the service of the individual. In the children's eyes the police exist to control, and to prevent, to catch criminals and make sure that they are punished. The police might be necessary, and be fighting for good, but they are seen as fighting, nevertheless. The police are associated with the need to control.

> 'They have to . . . well . . . go round the streets checking people aren't doing anything . . . crimes . . . and to see it doesn't happen again, take special precautions and try and stop crime.' *(girl, 10)*

> 'I think the police are trying to stop people being silly and breaking the law . . .' *(boy, 9)*

Given all the different laws that exist, and increasing powers, from the control of riots to checking cars, it is significant that the police are associated with prevention, with keeping an eye on things.

'They're trying to stop people getting killed and that.' *(girl, 10)*

Their role is a central one in maintaining the authority or the law.

'Well, they have to make sure that everybody does the right things.' *(girl, 10)*

Given this idea of control, the policing of other people's behaviour, it is not surprising that children assume that policemen spend much of their time chasing criminals. Policemen are not only there to prevent things happening, but there to catch the culprits after the event, so that they might be punished. The police are in the business of prevention and punishment, not only to:

'Stop people from doing anything wrong, like stealing things.' *(girl, 9)*

but

'The police usually catch them . . . I think they do a good job there to stop them.' *(girl, 9)*

The role that children readily associate with the policeman includes that of the detective, as well as that of the preventer of wrong-doing.

'They go out to car crashes and catch thieves, and track them down and things like that.' *(girl, 11)*

'They have to catch criminals . . . bad people. At night they sometimes break into your houses and steal things and they sometimes kill people. They get caught by the police.' *(boy, 7)*

In the police force's own definition of their role, the need to catch criminals often outweighs the need to help people; prevention of crime is a more immediate and more urgent need than the more leisurely aspects of courtesy, although children are still aware that one part of the job does not altogether prevent normal and helpful relations.

'Well, they have to find people who murder people and things like that . . . Yes, if you get lost you can always go to them.' *(girl, 10)*

Much of the work that police do, in tracing and catching criminals, has little to do with the general public. They are seen to be involved not just in maintaining the law but in doing so in specific ways:

> 'I think they should try and get as many people as they could and put them in gaol.' *(girl, 10)*

Children are clearly aware of the different roles of the police, not only in the mixture of general help and fighting criminals and rioters, but in different types of prevention that they are involved in, from catching speeding cars to arresting rapists. They are aware of the complexities of the role:

> 'Well, some policemen just go around the streets, and some policemen just go around the motorways and catch people speeding, and some of them are at the office — the police station.' *(girl, 9)*

> 'They have to help people . . . and guide traffic and everything on the roads, sort out murders that happen and things like that.' *(girl, 11)*

But the idea of symbolizing the strength of the law, by prevention and punishment, still persists. The police are there to make sure that people do not follow their natural tendencies; to put down riots, stop people being violent and make sure that all obey the traffic laws. There is no element of terror in this, but a sense that without the police there would be no law; that law is not a natural thing but something which has to be imposed. Prevention is essential.

> 'They have to try and prevent fights in the street and people going round trying to shoot everybody.' *(boy, 10)*

The image of the police that children bring to mind, apart from their helping, is of a powerful force that needs to be there to fight crime and violence. If there is one image that springs to mind in children's minds it is not of the village constable, nor of the detective, but of a mass of police officers, protected by their shields, against a horde of rioters or football hooligans. In this fight against rioters, policemen have the initial sympathy of children. Just as the police are found 'helpful' so they are seen to be fighting on the good side.

> 'Making sure riots don't start and things.' *(girl, 10)*

But even whilst they are approved of in preventing more violence, it is recognized that they also succumb to it.

> 'Sort of fights and things, robberies, murders all sorts of things. They help a lot. At riots and things they hurt other people. I think they're trying to stop other people but . . . when they're doing that they can hurt other people.'   *(girl, 10)*

Although clearly seen to be necessary, and in the right, and despite being supported by the power of law, the association of policemen with fighting pervades the children's responses.

> 'They help the riot. They try and stop it . . . They sometimes make it worse.'   *(girl, 8)*

> 'They join in the fight to stop them.'   *(boy, 10)*

Children are clear that the police need to fight, even if they do so in a good cause.

> 'They want to show them . . . they're fighting for peace . . . they're on the side of them. They want to show them the policemen are their friends.'   *(boy, 9)*

> 'Because when there's something like a riot, they're always there.'   *(boy, 9)*

The picture that children retain of the police is as a symbol of the power of law maintained by force, which suggests that the police face an uphill task — a battle rather than a consensus. The police are marked out not only by being on the side of the law, or by their uniform, but by their equipment.

> 'Um, they have to wear those special shields because . . . to stop them getting hit themselves. They get hold of the rioters to drag them off or something.'   *(girl, 10)*

> 'They have to get those riot shields and fight the people at the football grounds.'   *(boy, 8)*

The police force is seen by children not only as helpful, on the right side in the battle for peace, but as beleaguered. They are often pictured in difficult circumstances, fighting football hooligans, try- ing to control pickets, and confronting riots. This suggests to chil- dren that wherever there are many policemen there is a likelihood of violence. The massed array of policemen, as distinct from the individual policeman, is a sure sign of trouble; they are so much a sign of violence that a number of children begin to assume that their presence *causes* violence, that, however innocently, they act as *agents provocateurs*. Children know that the police are themselves not universally popular. Those who are rioting see the police as fair game.

> 'They might think it's making it worse because it's the police who cause what the police are trying to stop. They are against the police and so they try to do it even more.' *(girl, 9)*

But the police are seen to provoke violence both by preventing people doing what they want to do, and by over-reacting to them.

> 'I think they are making it worse in a way because they're stopping them from having drinks.' *(boy, 10)*

> 'I think they make things worse a bit. I think they have too many at one place.' *(girl, 9)*

Even if justified — 'It's the rioter's fault' — the police are assumed to be just as violent as those they are trying to control.

> 'Sometimes they over-react in big crowds of people.' *(girl, 11)*

When a large number of police are seen to gather children suggest that it is inevitable that there will be violence:

> 'Ring up the other police on the radio. Attack all people that are like pickets and things like that, if there is any fights or things like that or burglaries . . . Because most of the time they start the fights . . . Yes, they start the fights because once there's picketers about they go and hit them, trying to get them away and then the war starts.' *(boy, 9)*

This is not to suggest that children sympathize with any kind of riot. The interviews show that they have no sympathy at all for 'hooligans' of any kind. Nevertheless, the police are seen to be not only in a difficult position, but adding to their own difficulties.

> 'They do their best, but it's difficult. Well, they're trying to stop it, you know, while they're trying to stop it, but they're just going, they're just causing the fight because they're sort of . . . you know the people, the fans go, "Ah right, here come the police, let's go at them," and that's how they start fighting.' *(boy, 10)*

> 'Sometimes they come in at the wrong time. Sometimes they get people really annoyed and then the people who get annoyed get even more and

start fighting. They're not always wonderful the whole time. I think that perhaps some young people who've just joined in think that they're the police and that they can keep law and order and that they can boss everyone around. I think that that's not right. They are supposed to help people, not just get them all annoyed.' *(girl, 10)*

Time and again children cited cases of the police not only being caught up in violence, but provoking it: 'being a bit too tough on some people'. They are aware of the association between the police and plastic bullets, between the police and accidental death. One must remember that despite the imagery with which the police are depicted, children do not assume that the police are in any way enemies. They are seen as servants of a necessary law, as emissaries of power — a power that children accept. Children do not have an optimistic or sentimental view of the role of the police. Nor do they assume that there is some kind of personal threat in the way the police use force for the prevention of riots. In a sense, what they see is impersonal. They accept that the force is necessary even as they delineate their association of force with violence,

'Because they're often forced to use force.' *(boy, 11)*

What stands out in the children's minds are images of the police, perhaps as seen on the news, in which they are not just being helpful.

'But sometimes they do go a bit mad 'cos the other day I was watching something and a man come over and hit these men on the head, then they went down and whacked him.' *(boy, 11)*

'Well, they give directions, but they're a pain to other people who are breaking the law . . . I remember in the news, one time, in South Africa, the policeman burst into a room firing a gun and fired shots and killed a baby. The policeman's on a charge now.' *(boy, 10)*

No amount of distancing in that memory prevents the impression of the police as a force which can, and does, cause violence as well as prevent it, even if it is justified in doing so.

One might assume that the children's view of the police as helpful people forced into the position of violence would suggest that they are put into impossible circumstances beyond their own control. But children do not only acknowledge that the police can be tough or unfair. They also expand on their assumption that the police can do wrong. They are not seen as knights in shining armour. However willing to be helpful, and however much they are locked into the good side of the State, they are also seen as suffering from the same ordinary temptations as anyone else. Most of the children accept that the police do wrong as well as good. Their attitude is equivocal rather than critical. It is as if they accepted that part of the policeman's lot was to make mistakes.

'Well, some things they do wrong, but not all. They're usually helpful. Well, they killed a lady but they didn't mean to so I don't think that's really wrong.' *(girl, 9)*

'Sometimes they do things wrong but most of the time I don't think they are.' *(girl, 10)*

Some of the mistakes that are associated with the police are not seen as accidents.

'Well, um, like where the blacks are. The police there killed blacks but sometimes they do things which are meaningless but they usually only do it because they think they are helping.' *(girl, 10)*

'Sometimes the police cause offence to people . . . breaking into their homes by mistake. Sometimes they're not [helpful]. Sometimes they hurt by mistake or sometimes on purpose.' *(boy, 10)*

'Sometimes I think they are a bit sort of overactive and they arrest people for no real reason.' *(boy, 10)*

Children assume that the police are capable of arresting the wrong people and being as violent as their adversaries. The question is whether these mistakes are purely accidental or a natural symptom of giving a body of people particular powers.

The police are seen to 'do wrong' not so much because they make mistakes in terms of false arrests, but as a consequence of toughness. And yet children assume that the police need to be rough, as the only way of standing up to the many outbreaks of violence in society. That they will be under attack is not questioned. Children assume that society will always be like that. The consequences are that the police must react.

'Well, I was watching the news yesterday and they said that a lady had been punched by a policeman, and I think sometimes they go a bit far by handling the people when they're rioting. But they have to be quite rough, otherwise they're not going to get anywhere.' *(girl, 10)*

If the main cause of children's equivocal reactions to the police is their association with force, and the natural consequences of human nature, an underlying suspicion of the police is that they not only make mistakes, but are as corrupt as any other group of people. A significant number of children say that the police are capable of breaking the law that they are there to uphold, and that they can do so more easily because of the position they are in.

> 'Like I've heard of people even bribing policemen not to tell them, and policemen themselves commit loads of crimes and they don't even get punished for this, and they've sworn oaths not to tell each other, and if they do the policemen themselves will have terrible fights, and the person who wants to be good and say that the other person has committed a crime will get themselves really painfully hurt. Policemen should get punished as well as other people should.' *(girl, 9)*

One of the most immediate examples of the policeman's propensity to break the law is the fact that they are sometimes caught drinking and driving. Given that children feel that the police are 'only human' and yet should give a good example, any hint that they are not following those rules that they impose is taken very seriously.

> 'I heard one of them had been drinking and driving.' *(boy, 11)*

> 'Some of the policemen aren't as good as people say. Like some policemen are being . . . one in Liverpool, I think it was, got done for drinking and driving.' *(boy, 10)*

Despite children's respect for the law, and their sense of its necessity, and despite their belief in policemen as the necessary guardians of the law, they do not assume that the police are perfect. Part of this contrast is their acceptance that the police have a tendency to follow their own whims — like drinking and driving — or being provoked into violence when they should overcome it. But children also suggest that even in their more impersonal upholding of the law the police can do wrong, that there are suspicious practices, like tampering with evidence.

> '. . . like when they say that someone was killed or something and they get people they think have done it and they haven't. Because they've got to find proof really.' *(boy, 10)*

The children do not suggest that this consists of any large-scale corruption but more a matter of slackness, of the desire to arrest anyone. This can be true at demonstrations:

'Well, they tell you where you are and which way you need to go and they sometimes direct traffic, you know, when it's a busy road . . . they arrest people when they're protesting and all they're doing sometimes is sitting there.' *(boy, 11)*

One of the shared assumptions amongst many of the children, less strong than their general support for the police, is that the police are not always successful. They see the difficulties policemen face, trying to subdue rioters, and see that despite riot shields and other equipment, they are on the defensive.

'The police don't seem to be doing very good. They've been trying their best but don't kind of, well the riots don't keep on stopping. All they do is kind of, well, just kind of hitting and trying to arrest them but they don't arrest many . . .' *(boy, 10)*

But that lack of success is at a very different level from the inability to respond to less visible or obvious kinds of crime. One or two children mention their experience of the police and the disappointment that not more is done to help.

At one level children accept that the police are essentially on the side of good:

'Sometimes they can do things wrong, mistakes and things, but not too much . . . I think they're very good.' *(girl, 10)*

At the same time the police are perceived to be forced into difficult circumstances:

'They have to tackle riot people and people who . . . well, arrest people . . . and stuff.' *(girl, 10)*

The result is that the majority of children share an ambivalent view of the police — as helpful but also as dangerous, as well-meaning, but tough.

'They're all right. Some cases they're good. Some cases they're bad. They're very good with burglaries, but not with the miners.' *(girl, 7)*

'. . . and they protect the Prime Minister . . . sometimes they're a bit rough, I think.' *(girl, 11)*

The reason that children think that the police can make mistakes is that they are 'only human', that they are people who are not above common temptations, placed in difficult circumstances. The tone that children use is kindly rather than frenetic.

'Sometimes they make a muff of it . . . someone always make mistakes.' *(boy, 10)*

'Well . . . everybody makes mistakes.' *(girl, 9)*

Only rarely is the suggestion given that the police either do or should try harder than others:

'Well, they're only people, so . . . but I think they try harder than other people sometimes.' *(girl, 10)*

Children view the police, then, as a necessary force which has all the virtue of helping people, all the dangers of being armed, all the provocation of being confronted by riots and all the dishonesty that children assume lies in most people:

'Yes, they're very helpful. They help little children if they are lost. No one's perfect. Everyone does something wrong, like sometimes they give false evidence. Sometimes they do things wrong like fire plastic bullets at people. That can kill them if it hits them in the heart or something, but most of the time they're just protecting themselves with riot shields and sometimes if . . . when a riot's in full swing they hit people with truncheons but what they've done to the police . . . there's sometimes no other way of controlling people except by force.' *(boy, 10)*

NOTES AND REFERENCES

1. The report of the Committee of Enquiry, *Discipline in Schools*, chaired by Lord Elton. London: HMSO, 1989, p. 170.
2. DES, *Our Policeman*. London: HMSO, 1988.
3. Cullingford, C. *Children and Television*. Aldershot: Gower, 1984.

CHAPTER 7
The Other Side of the Law

'Well, they're sort of ruling our lives. When we have a sort of free country we could do what we like as long as we don't get drunk and drive unsteady.' *(boy, 8)*

Children learn that the world is 'ruled', literally. Even before they enter school where the rules are many, they learn that there are certain expected standards, things they ought to do and even more things they ought not to. These rules vary in kind and intensity. Some rules are expectations of manners: it is better not to rush down corridors. Other rules have clear moral sanctions: thou shall not kill. Such a variety can cause problems. The sense of unfairness can arise from applying a punishment appropriate to one kind of rule to another. It is very hard to know exactly into which category an offence comes, since it is not only actions and the result of actions that must fit the moral law, but motivations behind such actions.

Such ambiguity about moral, social and legal codes affects the world outside school as well as the system within it. There are clearly some accidents that cause great harm, like a car crash, but were not due to any deliberate malice. And there are many actions which are punishable, and yet about which children retain their own, differing point of view, as in the case of wearing seat belts. They see the tension between individual freedom of action and the policing of a set of rules and regulations. They also see that such a tension is inevitable, that each of them has broken rules and will do so again. But if they observe characteristically bad behaviour in schools, they also are witnesses to bad behaviour at a far deeper level in the society around them. Some disasters might be the result of accident or natural causes, but many are criminal acts. The news and drama programmes are dependent on the existence of human wickedness.

It comes as no surprise to children that human beings have a natural propensity to wickedness. They take for granted that there will always be criminals and that there will always be a need to control them, that the legal system and the police force are a necessary bulwark against chaos. This sense of incipient anarchy derives from the fact that not all antisocial actions are due to criminal causes. Of all the destructive excitements presented on television, the most common are riots, whatever the cause. If the one sure way of drawing attention to a cause is to demonstrate, it follows that the greater the strength of feeling and the number of participants, the greater the possibility of violence. Hence children's image of the police controlling varieties of protest demonstrations, for peace or against a new tax, for censorship or against the police themselves.

The law is a necessary control over anarchy, but the desire for anarchic action is seen to continue unabated. Given the sense of a government that will not be persuaded through public opinion, children see some form of protest as legitimate publicity. If there is something about which people feel strongly:

> 'They could make a union thing . . . tell the Government that it could be dangerous. No notice; we don't know about those people.' *(boy, 10)*

> 'Attract people to come along and go on strike or something.' *(girl, 10)*

The power of the mass, as well as the image of confrontation, is constantly brought to children's attention, since it is what the media is looking for. It is often demonstrated on the news that publicity is gained for actions rather than words.

> 'Go against them, like the pickets, go against the laws about mining and coal business. If they get enough people and they start things up like the pickets and the miners.' *(boy, 8)*

Although children observe a number of organized demonstrations, they are also reminded of the incidents of rioting, almost for its own sake. The main symbol of such crowd behaviour for children is the violence of hooligans at football matches. A demonstration for a purpose seems to children understandable or even justifiable. This is partly why they maintain a suspicion of the police response. But children fail to see any justification in the behaviour of football fans. They are quite clear that certain kinds of violence are particularly associated with football. They would not expect to find such behaviour at, say, a horse-race, whatever the strength of feeling aroused by losing a bet.

> 'If you went to, say, like a horse-race and you betted on a horse and your horse didn't win and somebody else's next to your horse did, they don't want to start a riot there really, do they?' *(girl, 11)*

But the idea of football hooliganism is vivid. The football fan is seen as loud, quarrelsome and dangerous. When children talk about football matches they reveal a number of attitudes that underline their view of the world. Football hooligans are a kind of symbol, of a manic desire to cause harm and an excessive devotion to particular causes. Children view them with a mixture of exasperation and casualness. It is as if they accepted that football fans' tendency to violence is a natural part of their make-up and to that extent inevitable. But they also despised this tendency. The reasons for such behaviour at football matches are themselves despised as well as seen as inevitable. They do not use the word 'childish' for such behaviour but that is the word that adults would, ironically enough, use to decribe their reaction to such symptoms.

Football fans are seen as loud, quarrelsome and drunk. Children express an almost weary contempt for the tendency to behave in ways they have all witnessed through the media, until the children associate domestic football matches with violence.

> 'I think it's disgusting, because they get so excited. It's different for them because they're older and they've got . . . well, the kind of people who go to football matches are yobs and they're that kind of person.' *(girl, 10)*

'The kind of people' who go to football matches are symbols of how people behave given the opportunity. Because a large crowd is gathered together, the desire to cause an affray, to riot or 'cause trouble', is seen to be endemic. Children have witnessed examples both of the violence that arises from exasperation, and from unsuppressed passion, and the conflicts that seem to be enjoyed for their own sake. Riots at football matches encapsulate both. The desire to see a team win at all costs is combined with deliberate attacks on rival fans. Children perceive these collective instincts, given expression through partisanship, as a new phenomenon.[1]

'It's just stupid. Didn't used to in the olden days.' *(boy, 10)*

They also think that such behaviour is despicable.

'I don't mind watching it but I don't like being at football grounds itself. I think it's disgusting actually for people to act like that.' *(girl, 11)*

Football crowds are associated with a horde, over-excited and out of control. They are referred to as 'mad' and 'silly'.

'If they came to watch it, they should watch it and when it's finished just go away.' *(girl, 10)*

But football hooligans are not assumed to be a small minority. The association between fans and hooligans comes about because children have an image of a football match as a place where some kind of violence is likely to happen. They have witnessed reports of major disasters but they have also learned that the violence of football fans, before, during and after a match, is an everyday recurrence. They have learned that the police attend all matches in readiness and expectation of violent clashes. They know that rival fans are kept in separate sections behind bars. Even when there is what is nowadays called a 'peaceful and troublefree' game — twenty arrests — children perceive the tendency to violence, and the signs of violence.

'They shouldn't do all the vandalizing and writing over everything. The grounds are supposed to look nice.' *(boy, 10)*

It is not just the rioting that strikes children but the other symbols of a desire for violence. Football is the opportunity given to people to behave as they would wish to behave but are not always allowed to.

'I think it's stupid, the people who do it. Because there's a lot of stuff lying around and there's bars you can rip up.' *(boy, 8)*

The question remains why people should behave like this. Are they typical of what is possible in anyone, or a grotesque minority? From their answers children both dismiss the behaviour they observe, mostly through the news, as outrageous and alien, and accept it as something that other people actually do, even if they wouldn't do so themselves. They are more exasperated than puzzled by such behaviour, and feel it is generally inevitable.

The children suggest a number of reasons why football crowds include a tendency to break out in fighting. One reason is close to children's own experience: the fear and anger of losing. But the collective anger, where everyone is part of the mass, is a different kind of thing from individual fear. It smacks not of humiliation but an unwillingness to accept defeat.

> 'I think it's silly because it's only because their team didn't win and then the other team fights back so it just makes a bigger mess.' *(girl, 10)*

It is as if one kind of assertion grew on another, and as if each confrontation with a different point of view only made the original assertion more extreme.

> 'Well, no, because some people support other teams and they sort of boast that their team won and then they sort of get angry with them, sort of boasting and then they say other things and then they start punching and things like that.' *(boy, 10)*

All children understand well the strength of feeling that can be engendered in supporting a particular side. They are encouraged to have favourites from an early age, from favourite colours to favourite pop stars. The boys especially will assert the superiority of their favourite football side, often in a parody of the gestures they have seen fans make. They know that looking at a game of football from the point of view of one team creates a passion of pleasure or sense of injustice, curiously extreme second-hand emotions.

> 'It's just that they're bad losers. They can't stand to lose.' *(boy, 10)*

> 'Well, the way they're so violent and fight with each other . . . because they're upset about one team losing or another team winning. People shout out that one team's horrible and they just start throwing cans and things.' *(girl, 9)*

George Orwell, some time ago, warned of the dangers of partisanship at football matches and that far from fostering international understanding, football was likely to create strong antipathies to other nations.[2] But children see it as inevitable that domestic conflicts will arise.

The question remains whether children see this desire to boast and the resentment at the victory of opponents as true of a minority, or of all football fans, and whether the expression of such feelings in physical terms is incipient in such feelings. Children think that all will feel similar strains of joy or anger but that some will be more restrained in their expression. There are some whom children think will find any excuse to fight.

> 'I think that's stupid 'cos other people just go to watch the game and they just come in and if they lose they go mad and the rockers start fighting.' *(boy, 11)*

Partisanship and resentment at losing are the fuel that stokes the violence. Football fans are bad losers as well as having a tendency to riot.

> 'Like if their favourite team loses because the referee says something that isn't true, they all start throwing things.' *(girl, 10)*

> 'To attract attention or when there are different goals scored, fouls or people being sent off, and they disagree with it.' *(boy, 11)*

The assertiveness of behaviour is associated not so much with bombast as with anger and resentment.

> 'Because if it's somebody else's fault in the other team, they don't like it.' *(girl, 11)*

Football matches are seen to bring out violent tendencies. Children assume that the majority of fans welcome the opportunities that football gives them:

> 'They say there's one lot of troublemakers moving around.' *(boy, 11)*

> 'They just go to have a fight.' *(girl, 9)*

Violence is therefore expected. It is as if there were a natural connection between anger and fighting, and between supporting a club and attacking others.

> 'Well, if someone supports one football club and someone supports another, they throw bricks and things.' *(boy, 10)*

But children also associate the violence of football fans with drink. They have been imbued with many explanations of what takes place on football grounds and the question of drunkenness is one that is often put forward.

> 'Because they get drunk and silly and just because another team is there, they think their team is 5,000 times better; then they start getting

angry about it and they throw things at the other team. When they see the police, they think they are just butting in and they think they should mind their own business, but it is their business.' *(girl, 10)*

In such volatile circumstances the vision of the clash between teams of spectators is as strong as that between footballers on the field. Children assume that the connection between a tendency for violence and action is made by drink.

'Because they drink and take drugs and smoke and that and they go in a kind of fit where they keep drinking and they get cross with one another and they start rioting.' *(boy, 10)*

The blame for violence on drink is not only a theoretical position but one made strongly through visual examples:

'On television they showed close-up pictures of this man and he had tons and tons of bottles of beer by his side, which is really bad.' *(girl, 10)*

Drunkenness is not only seen as a cause for bad behaviour but as a symptom in itself. It is another way in which people behave badly.

'They're drunk and they all want to get attention.' *(boy, 10)*

It is another sign of what children call 'silliness'. It is as if the lack of properly controlled behaviour in football matches, as in the playground, is because of over-excitement, something both natural and 'mad'.

'Well, they just decide that they don't like to obey the laws and I think that's very silly, so they decide to disobey the laws and get drunk and things.' *(girl, 8)*

'Generally just muck things up occasionally.' *(boy, 10)*

Not that any of the children approve. Whilst bad behaviour is accepted as inevitable, it is not condoned. Those who fight, whether at football matches or not, are despised.

'I don't like that. There's no reason for it. If they come to a football match they should just watch it properly. There's no reasons for killing people.' *(boy, 9)*

Recognition of violence is coupled by annoyance. For this reason children acknowledge it as inevitable both that some people will behave in this way and that they should be prevented from doing so.

If it is a natural tendency to enjoy fighting then the answer is seen by children to lie not in education but in control. Children despise the behaviour of football hooligans and would wish there were many more means of preventing their behaviour. When children are asked whether there is any solution to the problems of football hooligans, their first reaction is that:

'They should get rid of them.' *(boy, 8)*

'They should stop it.' *(girl, 7)*

The suggestion is that if there are football matches there will also be trouble. The solution is either to control behaviour or not allow crowds to gather.

'They'll just have to stop football matches altogether. They just should not let people who are going in to go in.' *(girl, 9)*

'They probably have to not allow anybody to go to the football matches and put it on television so people can watch it instead of going.' *(boy, 10)*

'They can ban people from going to football matches.' *(girl, 9)*

This is the ultimate solution, demonstrating that there is no suggestion of possible changes in behaviour. But the more common solution that children put forward depends on greater crowd control. This is where they see the need for an even greater police presence. If spectators are not going to be banned, then they need to be policed. Children assume that football will continue to be a mass entertainment with a continuing element of hooliganism. The police therefore become an essential ingredient in football matches:

'The police should go up to them and stop them.' *(girl, 9)*

'I think they should send in a bit more police.' *(boy, 11)*

Indeed, it is even suggested that violence is partly caused by not having enough police.

'Well, really, I think it's useless because they pay the money to come and watch the football match and that's what they're asked to come and do — buy tickets — and when it ends up in violence there's not enough police around.' *(boy, 8)*

The rights of the normal football fan need protecting physically. But there are times when even that kind of control is seen to be inadequate.

'Well, they had quite a lot of police there didn't they? But they couldn't stop it. There's too many Liverpool supporters there.' *(boy, 10)*

Given the power of the masses and the sheer number of attempts to cause a riot, restraint is not seen as the only form of control. Punishment is contemplated not so much as a deterrent as an inevitable follow-up. If fans are made to pay fines it might have the long-term effect of keeping them away. But the main punishment is again seen as imprisonment.

'They should be sent to prison for a lifetime.' *(girl, 8)*

The hope of control lies with fierce sanctions, and with making certain that offenders are caught.

'They should continue what they are doing — putting cameras in and they should photograph the people who they can see and they should look for them.' *(girl, 9)*

And, once caught, they need to learn the consequences of their actions.

'I think they should be taken to a special place because they do, some of them, don't they? They take them to a special place where they're disciplined and made to obey and not break the law.' *(boy, 10)*

For most of the children, however, incarceration is not a question of retribution nor of any moral regeneration, but a simple pragmatic matter of restraining people from continuing to act in the same way.

'I think they should arrest them. I think they should send them off because otherwise if they don't . . . then they might get worse and then eventually some people could get hurt.' *(boy, 11)*

Restraint and punishment, both needing the operation of a large police force are, therefore, seen as the central bulwarks of the law of constraint and control. But children are also pragmatic about the need to control the behaviour of the football fans *in situ*. The operation of the police in ever-increasing numbers is not felt by children to be enough in itself. It needs to be supported by other practical means. One such is seen as the need to 'ban drinking'. If alcohol is depicted as one of the additional causes of bad behaviour it follows that it should be controlled.

'Well, before they go in they have to hand over their alcohol.' *(boy, 9)*

Some of the means of control can be quite elaborate.

'All the pubs should shut then . . . or they know that the fans are coming from a long way away. They should keep all the pubs along the way shut, or just don't let any strange, you know, the sort of persons who look as if they want trouble, in.' *(boy, 10)*

The sort of person who 'wants trouble' is seen to be at the heart of the problem. Recognizable they might be, but, like the poor, always deemed to be with us.

The shutting of pubs and the control of alcohol, however, is a minor part of the means of prevention and restraint suggested by children. Rivals have a strong tendency to fight, runs the argument, and they should therefore be kept away from each other, or at least controlled. Children observe all the means already taken to separate rival fans, and suggest increasing such means.

'People shout out that one team's horrible and they just start throwing cans and things . . . by having one team sit in one half of the stadium and the other on the other half and a fence kind of between them so that anything can't get across.' *(girl, 9)*

One wonders whether the ultimate solution might be to apply the same criteria to the footballers themselves. Meanwhile, control is achieved through ever-greater barriers to enforce separation.

'You could make the fences more better and stronger . . .' *(boy, 8)*

'Put electric fences up to stop them from climbing over.' *(boy, 10)*

Children elaborate on various kinds of separation, not only of rival gangs but of those who wish to watch the game peacefully.

'Have certain places that they're only allowed to go and other places that the people who want to go and enjoy it seriously can go and sit and have nobody to interfere with them.' *(girl, 9)*

In order that the crowd 'stay seated and be quiet' there needs to be not only separation but elaborate means of holding them in, whether by electric fence, or by designing new types of stadia.

105

'They should make a big barbed wire fence all made out of barbed wire and then they make it just a big kind of curve round with two doorways at the end that leads in and out. That would stop them.' *(boy, 10)*

'What I think they should do is sort of put them in little houses. It's brick and then there's a big glass sheet so you can see through and they can't get out.' *(girl, 10)*

The children imply that there will always be football hooligans, and that if matches continue to be played some means of control needs to be developed. It suggests that they see the craving for rioting and fighting as being deep-seated as in certain animals, except that it is for its own sake. The imagery of football holds a vision of social control, with increasingly complex machinery concerned with detection. Some children suggest the stadia of the future will have the sophisticated devices of airports.

'They could have a sort of detection, a metal detector, sort of like the airports have to find metal objects and stuff like that so they can detect guns and metal items and stuff and get them out. They take hand pistols . . .' *(boy, 10)*

The likening of hooligans to terrorists is telling. It implies an equal determination to find a means of doing harm. Riots are therefore not only envisaged as spontaneous outbreaks of anger and disappointment, fuelled by drink, but as deliberate acts by those who like that kind of thing. As at airports, attention therefore needs to be paid to detecting what people bring with them, whether drink or weapons.

'. . . well, I don't go to football matches but I do know someone who does go a lot. I think they ought to have special checks on everybody all the time and they're not allowed to smoke or anything. They've just got to sit there with all their . . . they have to check everything, like they have in aeroplane checks and that.' *(boy, 9)*

As behaviour gets worse, so does the need to constrain become the greater. Children believe that the answer to violence lies not in curing the participants but in preventing them from manifesting their natural symptoms. But this growth in violence affects not only the football fans who become hooligans but also the forces of law and order there to control them. It is as if there were two growing armies, of law and order, as well as rioters.

'There ought to be more of them around now. There ought to be a lot more of them on football pitches. There ought to be laws.' *(boy, 10)*

The police are seen to be caught up in violence, even when they are not provoking it.

'I don't think it's a very good idea, them going round on horses getting hurt and the police getting hurt.' *(girl, 9)*

The police are seen to be a target for rioters. On the one hand, they are acknowledged as absolutely necessary. But, ironically, they are also seen to have become part of the violence. For the fighting begins to affect all people, whether in the picket line or in the stadium.

'Well, the police come and sort of have a fight with the ones that went wrong.' *(girl, 8)*

There is no question in children's minds where the guilt for the violence lies.

'It's definitely not the police's fault. It's the rioters' fault.' *(girl, 11)*

'They shouldn't fight with the police really 'cos they're the people who are trying to stop all this.' *(boy, 10)*

Nevertheless the central role of the police lies in fighting, not just crime but every outbreak of violence. They are up against crowds of passionate people driven by hate, whether gathered in the picket line or in the football stadium. And this force needs to be used.

'Well, they might have to hit people or something, but that's only because they're doing really stupid things.' *(girl, 10)*

Such use of force in these circumstances in particular leads children to believe that there are times when the police inevitably overdo it. They are so much part of the picture during any serious riot that their role is almost ambiguous.

'Some of the people are right who are doing the violence and I think that they arrest too many people, but if they try and attack them, they have the right to arrest them.' *(boy, 10)*

'At riots and things they hurt other people. I think they're trying to stop other people, but . . . when they're doing that they can hurt other people.' *(girl, 10)*

The sense of incipient universal violence, even if actually provoked by a 'crazy' minority, nevertheless affects the whole of society. It is not enough to build electric fences and use detection devices. The police need to be on hand to force control and arrest people who will resist. And then one form of violence spills into another.

> 'When riots are occurring they sometimes hit some people for no reason.' *(boy, 10)*

> 'I think they make it worse, really. They're there and if the people don't like them, they start fighting with the police.' *(girl, 11)*

In considering the relationship of football hooligans to the police, the image of society that is suggested is one of greater violence and more savage control, larger crowds of rioters and more strenuous punishment. Even when children insist on the need for more police, and even as they see how the police must use force, there is an underlying ambiguity in their attitude, which arises from the sense of increasingly physical solutions to problems. After all the emphasis of support to the law is not an argument but punishment. Sophisticated equipment adds better means not of persuasion, but detection. To the use of the horse in riots is added the use of plastic bullets.

> 'Firing plastic bullets is wrong. That can harm people.' *(boy, 9)*

> 'Well, the police have to come out and sometimes they use plastic bullets and they start getting violent because they don't want the other ones to get violent either.' *(girl, 10)*

The greater the means of control, the greater the chance of violence. And this is part of entertainment. So the view of the world as a place full of hooligans encompasses a world in which even the forces of law and order are caught up in extreme events, and in which they too can make mistakes.

> 'Yes, but if the police shoot somebody that isn't doing it, I think they should be put in prison for that.' *(girl, 10)*

And prison, as the means of controlling all who do wrong, encompasses all.

NOTES AND REFERENCES

1. Marsh, P. *Aggro: The Illusion of Violence*. London: Dent, 1978.
2. Orwell, G. 'The sporting spirit,' in *Collected Essays, Journalism and Letters*, Vol 4. London: Penguin, 1970, pp. 61–64.

CHAPTER 8
The Army of the Unemployed

'They should be working harder to get jobs.' *(boy, 9)*

The imagery of society might be presented in a simplistic way, but children interpret what they observe in ways which are anything but simplistic. Children's knowledge of the structures of society and the nature of power and control is extensive and firm. Whilst there might be constitutional niceties that remain unexplained, the way that society as a whole fits together is clear. Children acknowledge the forces of order, and witness the extent to which parts of society are against such order for one reason or another. If they see society divided between order and disorder, they also see society divided between the rich and poor, those who are successful and those who are not. Children do not convey any romantic sense of perfect contentment. Protest and unhappiness are always before them.

Children also have a realistic sense of what societies do about the unemployed. Before their attitudes are explored it should be made clear that they are based on knowledge. They know that the purpose of taxation is to support social security benefits as well as the fabric of education, transport and defence. They know about the problems of the economy. And they know about the divisions that such problems create, not only between politicians, but between sections of society. Pictures of rioting or football hooliganism might make more of an impact, but children also know about the unemployed. They are familiar with the apparatus of provision:

'They go to the Jobcentres and ask for a job.' *(boy, 8)*

and the fact that it is a government responsibility to support people until they find a job. They are also aware of the problem of low wages and the connection between low wages and unemployment benefit.

'Some people get paid less than what they get on the dole.' *(boy, 11)*

When children refer to the 'dole' there is a sense of disparagement as if it were easy, unearned money.

'They go on the dole . . . they get money.' *(girl, 11)*

The government is seen as playing the part of a charitable agency.

'The Government give them some money, don't they?' *(girl, 9)*

Those who need the money are in a position of some dependency. When the need is greater, more money has to be found. Children realize that the money has to come from some budget; that there is never enough simply to give out largess.

'Mrs Thatcher could talk to the businesses and tell them to give money out.' *(boy, 10)*

The government is seen as helping to raise money, cajoling others into action, as well as providing Jobcentres and solutions to the problem by creating jobs. But there is an underlying sense of the need for the rich to take pity on the poor, secure in the knowledge that they are being charitable. The children might pity the unemployed but it does not follow that they respect them. They reiterate the assumption that the unemployed are either not capable of finding jobs, not wishing to do so, or not trying hard enough. At the same time children wonder why the unemployed are willing to accept these 'gifts'.

The system of social security is not described as a right of individuals to expect support from society, nor seen as a way of redistributing wealth. It is seen as heavily dependent on the willingness of some to give money to others, more specifically:

'The rich should help the poor.' *(girl, 8)*

Indeed, the kinds of help and support that the unemployed are considered to need are put into palpable terms like food, clothing and housing.

'Some kind people might be able to give them a bit of a home.' *(girl, 9)*

'Give them food, money, clothes . . .' *(boy, 9)*

Just as the decisions made by the government are described as being made by personalities, by individuals, so the money to support the unemployed is not some anonymous abstraction but belonging to richer people. The system depends on the willingness of the rich to be generous.

> 'If there's kind of some, they're very rich but they don't kind of go on about it or anything but they give money to the poor. If everyone did that, it wouldn't be unfair, but quite a lot of people who are rich, they don't give any money to. It is a bit unfair. Nothing can be done about it.' *(girl, 9)*

Not all children feel that nothing can be done about it. Indeed, one boy feels that a measure of social action, based on historical principles, should be taken, if only it did not conflict with other laws:

> 'Well, steal, like Robin Hood did. You could steal some money from the rich and give it to the poor. But it's wrong to steal.' *(boy, 8)*

This is one version of social security.

The unemployed are seen as the poor. Their unemployment is seen as being partly their own fault. This underlying lack of sympathy is expressed by all children, including those whose own parents are unemployed. The reason for this lack of sympathy is that they have an underlying belief that all could gain jobs if they wanted to. After all, children themselves see the purpose of schooling as the acquisition of a job. The thought that they might not get one, that all that labour might be wasted, is inimicable to them.[1] They could not equate the striving for qualification with having no palpable outcome. So the unemployed are assumed to lack the will to find a job, to be unwilling to travel for a job, or to prefer not to have a job and live off charity — the dole.

The question, then, is what can be done. One clear answer for children lies in some kind of self-help. Whilst they hint that each person is responsible for himself they also suggest that unemployment is temporary. For some there might be pragmatic solutions.

> 'They could sell things.' *(girl, 9)*

> 'Well, you could suggest to them where you think they should go . . . sell things, furniture, jewellery.' *(girl, 7)*

All solutions of the individual kind are, however, seen as temporary. The assumption they make is that employment *can* be found, that if enough effort is made, the solution lies there. Children therefore conclude that there are some who keep trying, and some who do not.

'They should get themselves employed, try and find a job. Try and make money. The police could help them.' *(girl, 8)*

'Go to another place where they can work. They should try and get a job.' *(boy, 9)*

The abiding sense is that if they 'keep trying' they will find some kind of work, and that they should find anything to avoid being on the dole. It is not only the police who (uniquely) are seen to have a role; children feel that there is advice available, as in Jobcentres:

'Probably get some people to tell them what they could do.' *(boy, 8)*

Some children have personal experience of people out of work and what they did about it.

'My Mum had a friend who was unemployed but who managed to get a job.' *(girl, 7)*

The views about those who fail:

'Quite a lot of them, they want a job and they can't find one.' *(boy, 11)*

are in the context of a fundamental belief that jobs are available to those that really want them.[2]

Given the knowledge about government action, however privately based, children see that there are other solutions to the problem of unemployment. The individual might well be able to find a job, given enough determination and education, but children are nevertheless aware that there remain a significant number of people who are out of work. For them the solution that matches their determination to succeed lies in the creation of more jobs. This is seen as being a responsibility of the government, or some depersonalized agency referred to as 'they'.

'Some people are leaving school and you hear on the news that they don't have jobs and they sort of distract people and do things to the towns. It's not really getting any better. They should try and provide more jobs or have somewhere for them to go to that's interesting.' *(girl, 10)*

The most palpable form of action that can be taken to ease the problem of unemployment is the creation of more Jobcentres, revealing a certain amount of faith in their efficiency.

> 'I think they should open up more Jobcentres for them.' *(boy, 9)*

But if that doesn't work, or if there are not enough, as if Jobcentres had jobs to give, then there is always voluntary work with the most visible of agencies.

> 'They go to the Jobcentre; if there isn't any, ask the police if they want helpers.' *(boy, 9)*

Children perceive the need for occupation. We can again and again detect a link in their comments between idleness and crime. If people have nothing better to do they will 'distract' themselves. Whether the occupation is a job or voluntary work doesn't matter so much if the alternative is to find time for 'rioting'. Children's dislike of the unemployed derives partially from this association. But there are still unemployed who remain a problem. The system of taxes that provides social security is acknowledged but not as strongly approved of as self-help. The question for some children is whether there are more fundamental solutions. It is the poor and unemployed who also tend to be homeless.

> 'Some people haven't got houses and they could spend more on houses and they've got places for homeless people but they should spend more on those things . . . They don't need any more money because they've got houses and clothes and their family.' *(girl, 11)*

Here we have a mixture of solutions: selling things, nurturing the poor, and creating employment. But the tone is again one in which the real solution lies in self-help, in immediate and pragmatic terms. Only one child analysed some underlying causes for unemployment and suggested that there might simply not be enough jobs for full employment.

> 'I think that perhaps they might be able to find a way to solve unemployment. And I think it's silly that other countries try to sell us robots. They go into factories and do jobs which people can do. I'm not saying that you shouldn't use combine harvesters, because it would be silly just using scythes, but America is making robots that can be used in Mcdonald's, and I think that if England started trying to get those it

would be very silly because some people really enjoy doing that. Or if
you had an electric dustman.' *(girl, 10)*

Having a job keeps people occupied, and occupation is seen as preventing crime. But jobs are also thought of as pleasurable. Children
do not talk about jobs as chores to be undertaken for money. It
seems that they might have heard protests about pay and conditions, but never complaints about the idea of working. What they
do know about, often from personal experience, is the difficulty of
being unemployed.

> 'He used to drive a lorry but he doesn't now. He's still got a lorry but
> he doesn't go out in it. He just works round the yard and things.'
> *(girl, 8)*

> 'Because people who do have jobs, they just get . . . like my Dad used
> to be a builder and all the people who came, just one Sunday morning
> . . . all sacked, my father, who was his best mate, my uncle . . .'
> *(boy, 8)*

The personal knowledge of the effects of being sacked, however,
does not create any greater sympathy for the unemployed, or hate
of employers, despite their awareness of a society divided in terms
of money and possessions. The feeling that prevails is that if one job
is lost then another is available, and that sheer determination will
lead to success.

> 'Some of them don't really try to get one.' *(girl, 9)*

> 'Some of them don't even want to work. They live on the dole.'
> *(boy, 10)*

Sometimes there is a reason for not wanting a job.

> 'My Mum's unemployed. Well, she could get a job but she'd get less
> money from that job than she would from the council, so there's no
> point.' *(girl, 8)*

> 'Dad. He's not very worried because he's doing our house.' *(boy, 8)*

The dangers of unemployment are seen not just as a matter of
financial insecurity but as a matter of boredom. The unemployed
should actively seek jobs because they might otherwise find less
respectable occupations.

> 'And they just get really fed up and they just . . . and they just start
> rioting. They should try to look for work, to get a job and try to

decorate their houses, for something to do. Something to do while you're waiting for a job, stuff like that. The Government gives out to them, the people who are unemployed, just the odd couple of quid like.' *(boy, 10)*

The advice to be given, beyond finding a job, is to keep occupied. But the children also detect some of the bitterness that goes with unemployment. They are not from a part of the United Kingdom with a massive unemployment problem, although they are aware of what is going on from the news. If they do not express great sympathy for the unemployed it is partly because they see the problem sometimes in individual and sometimes in collective terms. The individual is deemed to be able to find a job if he wants it. Seen in larger terms unemployment becomes a different problem, more dangerous but also solvable, in the creation of more Jobcentres, for instance. But children are also aware of larger forces — like the introduction of robotics — that threaten jobs. They are aware, for example, of the threat to seamen and shipowners in South-East England from the building of the Channel Tunnel.

'Well, they probably think that they're going to lose all their business and their business will all go to waste.' *(girl, 10)*

'They obviously wouldn't want it because they would be out of a job.' *(girl, 10)*

'And then they'll have the ferry people; they'll put even more people on the job lists.' *(boy, 11)*

Unemployment can be seen to have all kinds of causes. But the unemployed are regarded as a large social problem, like football hooliganism, at once inevitable and needing a solution. There is some sympathy for the unemployed, if sparse. There is no sympathy for those who go on strike. Children understand protest and acknowledge the helplessness people feel when they cannot make their voices heard. But strikes are associated with riots. Whatever the cause, the images in children's minds are affected by picket lines and confrontations, with all the elements of violence that attend newsworthy demonstrations. One reason for the dislike of strikers is the irony of the contrast with those unemployed who are actively seeking a job.

'I think it's a bit selfish really when there's people looking for a job to go on strike wanting more money.' *(girl, 11)*

The general feeling against strikes is militant. Children think that there are other ways of bargaining for more pay.

> 'People striking for money . . . is rubbish. They earn money.' *(boy, 8)*

The assumption is that every strike is for more money rather than a protest against working conditions. Striking is associated with greed.

> 'I think they should be told off for doing it.' *(boy, 9)*

> 'They shouldn't really go on strike.' *(girl, 8)*

Just as the unemployed should seek another job, so should people discontented with their work.

> 'It's silly going on strike. Go to another place where they can work.' *(boy, 9)*

To go on strike is seen to be counterproductive, both to colleagues and themselves. Children suggest that people should be forced to go back to work and that strikes should be forbidden. Teachers shouldn't strike, 'because children are missing their lessons'. (girl, 8). Certain groups of workers, like miners, are deeply associated with strikes.

> 'The miners will keep coming back to strike.' *(girl, 7)*

But never is the idea of a strike seen as being sensible or efficient or successful. Strikes are 'silly' and children feel there should be, as with unemployment, some means of dealing with the problem.

> 'I think it's stupid because the whole country has to suffer. And so do they because they're not getting any money or anything. Go back to work. They ought to go to court, really. Settle it up between judges.' *(boy, 10)*

Children assume that there are more sensible methods of settling a dispute than striking. The answer to the individual's problem is a different job; the answer to the collective dispute is greater dialogue. They rarely connect the strike with a means of protest, despite the fact that they recognize the potential power of a mass of people. One of the means of demonstrating disagreement with a law or a condition is to strike.

'Attract people to come along and go on strike or something.'
(girl, 10)

Here the strike is associated with the picket line. But the motivation for striking is nearly always seen as greed. Whilst the most vivid image of strikers is when they are in a state of conflict with the police, the idea of the strike is not associated with any political idea. Just as the unemployed might have nothing better to do, so that they cause trouble, so the striker is motivated in a way that children despise.

Again, the next question is, what can be done? The immediate advice to those who wish to go on strike is 'don't'. Instead, they should continue to work and find other means of negotiation.

'They should carry on working. Complain.'   *(boy, 9)*

'I think you should just go and ask for a raise. Or maybe work harder and you might get more.'   *(girl, 9)*

'I think they should go on working. By working harder, sometimes. And by asking the Government.'   *(boy, 7)*

It does not follow that children think that complaints will lead to immediate action. Nevertheless, the idea that harder work that is rewarded with more money can be demonstrated, suggests that people get what they deserve. Any alternative is better than striking. Children suggest that negotiations are crucial.

'They could all talk to them. Persuade the person to do more for the company.'   *(boy, 10)*

'I'd go to the person in charge and tell him to do something about it.'
(boy, 11)

Striking is seen as no answer to the desire for more money, partly on pragmatic grounds. Strikers seem to have even less money which appears to contradict the fact that it is the desire for more money which is always seen as the motivation.

'It depends on what they go on strike for. For more money . . . I don't know. I wouldn't go on strike. I'd just stay there and keep working. Even if the money was bad you'd just be losing more money if you do strike. Go and have a straight talk with the manager. There is not much that can be done except for opening new workplaces.   *(boy, 9)*

Strikers are despised not just because of the contradictions of their position but because they are seen as motivated by greed. Whilst the unemployed seem to lack determination to do better, strikers should submit more easily to their conditions. People go on strike because:

> 'They want more money. And I don't think they should give it to them.' *(boy, 10)*

But even if they are not being paid a fair wage, striking is not seen as the answer. Some might think:

> 'They're not getting enough money.' *(girl, 8)*

But all accept that there are other means of settling grievances than strikes.

Many of the children's attitudes to strikes, the reasons for them, their way of dealing with them, and their general disapproval of them are summed up in a sense of the reality of actual events, and the difficulties of doing anything about it. They might associate work with the fulfilment of a particular job, and they might assume that it is always possible to change jobs, but when confronted about what they would do to change the circumstances, they generally realize how helpless they are. It is as if strikes were a part of a social phenomenon, about which something could be done but somehow will always need to be suppressed. The children have grown up in a continuing atmosphere of riots, of strikes and unemployment. They have many ideas about their causes, but share a strong distaste for the manifestations of these causes, to the extent that they feel that the answer lies in suppressing the manifestations rather than exploring the causes. Below the complex ideas towards strikes lies a fundamental realization that the circumstances are not fair but there is little that can be done about it. Instead, the need is for greater control.

NOTES AND REFERENCES

1. Cullingford, C. *The Inner World of the School*. London: Cassell, 1991.
2. *Ibid*. Chapter 2.

CHAPTER 9
Society and the Individual

'It won't ever change because if the police can't control the place, it's going to get worse.' *(boy, 10)*

Children possess a deep-seated desire for order. This begins with the need to make perceptual sense of the world they are in, and continues with the development of language, in the fundamental need to categorize. Order, a coherent system, a structure of classification, is a necessary part of children's perception of the world. But order can also become a simplistic systematization. Prejudices are formed from applying a series of rules to all cases. A rigid mental 'set' can become so hardened that it becomes impossible to change. A sense of order is a necessary means of understanding the world, and a potential limitation. To understand children's approach to the rules of society it is necessary to understand this tension between the strength and limitations of a sense of order.

Children first perceive systems in social terms in the order, or disorder, of their own homes and in the behaviour of their parents. They soon know whether the adult means what she says and soon detect inconsistencies. They learn to prefer rules that are firm and clear, and approach schools with an acceptance of the need for rules. It is then at school, their first social centre, that children observe rules in action, including the tension between the idea and the reality, between the system and its interpretation. In school, children also observe how rules are applied differently to different people, how people bypass, avoid or ignore rules and the sanctions that support them. They also experience unfairness.

Children's realization of the need for rules and their perception of the difficulty of applying them consistently also affects their views of society. Their attitudes to the police, to politicians and to lawyers show how deeply they accept the significance of their power, and how little they assume that such power is wielded in a way that is always perfect, always immune from criticism. Children both accept the realities and criticize them. What else could they do? They see advertised, as it were, on television, all the faults of party politicians, the quarrels between them, and ever-increasing concerns with the corruption of the police and the prejudices of judges. They might not have been taught in detail how these systems work but come to fundamental conclusions from what they observe. They know that they have the right to protest. They feel secure in the freedom of being able to write letters and talk to people, and in the democratic belief that if enough people agree about an issue then that gives greater attention to it. But they also feel cynical about the result of protest. They observe the slowness of change. They watch the unresponsiveness of political leaders. And, above all, they see the forces of law and order resisting change.

Children's sense of order and disorder is strong. They are constantly reminded of the wilfulness of human nature, not only in school, through bullying and the breaking of rules but in society through the way it is presented on the news. There was a time when it was considered that children were optimistic, in the sense of having a sunny world view, believing that all things work for good, that people in positions of authority are fitted for their role.[1] Children might have a strong sense of humour, and a strong desire to make things work. They might also look at their own progression with hope and optimism, with openness to change. But it does not follow that they are optimistic about other people, about society or the individual. They are too aware of what goes on, and are pragmatic about general human behaviour.

Children reiterate the need for clear and strict laws. They accept the necessity of the police force in enforcing the law. This is because they also accept that there is a natural propensity for people to disobey the laws and that it is through threat of punishment that many people are prevented from behaving in an unrestrained manner. They both despise those who are violent and accept that some people have a natural desire to be violent that needs controlling. With such a need for authority and control, the question is what would happen if there were no system of justice and punishment. Would the better part of human nature take over? Do the police merely provoke difficulties? Or are people so inclined that only rules constrain them? On this question children are of one mind.

> 'I think we should have laws because otherwise if people were just allowed to do anything people are just going to be robbing banks, and stuff like that. You need something to deter people from doing bad things.' *(boy, 9)*

It is, of course, not the rules that constrain but the enforcement of the rules, through the police.

> 'If the police can't control the place, it's going to get worse.' *(boy, 10)*

Control is seen as an essential ingredient of society. It is as if all the mechanisms of organization and communication were a kind of policing. Children do not suppose that all the usual functions of social life, both public and private, would continue if there were not a system of control. This belief in the importance of constraint does not apply only to the small minority of people children might associate with hooliganism. The sense of the explosiveness of a society without strict rules is all pervading. It is as if everything, the whole country, would be out of control.

> 'Everything would be kind of messed up and everything would be lost because people might steal things and people kill everyone.' *(girl, 8)*

> 'The country would just go out of control.' *(boy, 10)*

Before children become specific about what needs controlling, they express a general fear of chaos, of the unleashing of manic forces bent on destruction. Whilst some of the images of destruction that come to mind are private and individual — single acts rather than organized and collective ones — the sense of disorder is pervasive, as if violent tendencies were universal.

> 'Everybody would sort of get out of hand and a lot of people would be killed and things.' *(girl, 11)*

> 'The country would go to pieces.' *(boy, 11)*

As with children's perceptions of the role of the police, there are different levels at which chaos would be manifest. The result of abandoning control over the way people are made to obey traffic rules is seen to be an automatic rise in the number of car accidents, as well as more serious crimes.

> 'Well, people would kill themselves when they haven't put their seat belts on.' *(girl, 10)*

'There'd be crashes every day.'   *(boy, 10)*

Not only are there seen to be constraints over crime but over the way people go about their business. One might have thought that self-interest would foster attention being paid to the Highway Code, that drivers would continue to drive with care. But children assume that the presence of the police is a central factor in preventing 'a lot more accidents'. They make a distinction between the conventions of driving, like driving on the left, and the rules that can be broken, like speed limits and drink/drive laws, which they feel would be broken as often as people could get away with it.

The need for prevention also covers more serious crimes. What is depicted as incipient civil unrest would present itself in a number of ways, including burglary.

'The country would go to pot. There'd be people mugging people all the time and there'd be people stealing from shops the things like that.' *(girl, 11)*

It is as if there were a large criminal class waiting for the chance to go 'burgling'. This view of society is anything but a peaceful one, as if the natural urges of citizens need constant constraint.

'There'd be much more rapes and that lot.'   *(boy, 8)*

But the sense of criminality is not confined, in children's eyes, to a small number of people. They suggest that there could be an explosion of violence if there were no sanctions, and no police. They sense that everybody would be involved, especially in killing:

'Everybody would go around murdering everybody else.'   *(boy, 9)*

'There wouldn't be many people left and everything would be going wrong and there'd be lots of fights and killings and crashing and drunken people and everything like that.'   *(girl, 10)*

It is the sense of everyone being involved in mayhem that is so singular. Obviously 'everybody' can be a term as vague and as specific as 'they', when applied to an anonymous decision; 'You know what they have done?' But the term is used in a more all-embracing fashion:

'Everyone would just start fighting.'   *(girl, 9)*

It implies a deep-rooted belief in the incipient violence of society.

'People would just run riot and do anything and nobody could stop them.' *(boy, 10)*

Once unleashed these social forces would seem to be uncontainable:

'It would just get in a mess and everyone would be fighting and getting hurt.' *(girl, 10)*

No one suggests that things might be a little different, and that control is only necessary over the few. Children sense a more pervasive violence, not just centred on individual acts of murder or rape but in more general rioting:

'There'd be sort of riots everywhere and that.' *(boy, 10)*

'Lots of people would be getting hurt.' *(girl, 11)*

'We'd keep on having fights.' *(girl, 8)*

It is not only the minority of football fans, it appears, spoiling for a fight. Nor is it a matter of the idle unemployed finding something to do. The sense of the outbreak against the forces of law and order, if given the chance, is more widespread.

'Everyone would be running riot everywhere.' *(boy, 11)*

The system of law and punishment is therefore seen as a necessity to control not just a minority but society as a whole. 'Fighting' and 'rioting' cover a far larger spectrum of people and a more general source of the mass than specific crimes. Rioting is not seen as an outbreak of feelings of outrage or injustice *against* society, but an example of lack of social restraint. If it were not for an organized society, children feel, the world would be in chaos. They suggest that an immediate consequence of the lack of a police force would be a powerful and destructive urge towards violence that would involve everyone, victims as well as perpetrators.

'People would go around killing each other and being horrible and leave litter all over the place.' *(girl, 9)*

'Well, the world would be a disgrace. You'd have people running around killing each other.' *(boy, 9)*

Such is the collective view of human nature as a whole, as if the veneer of civilization were very thin. What are seen as highlights on television become the norm if there are no constraining forces.

'Everybody would be fighting and breaking the law and most probably get killed.'   *(girl, 10)*

'People would be going around killing each other or people would be getting drunk and then going along in a car and then crashing.'   *(boy, 11)*

Again and again children say 'everyone':

'Everyone would be killing everyone. Everything would be ruined. We wouldn't have many houses.'   *(boy, 9)*

One presumes that none of these children has any propensity to kill others, or riot. Their bleak picture of a society which could destroy itself is a context in which they see themselves. And they are aware of the possibility of being caught up in violence as victims, whether at a football match or in a riot. The sense of 'everyone' being involved includes all those who would be suffering.

'Everybody would be dying and everything would be going missing.'   *(girl, 9)*

'There'd be hardly any people left in the world.'   *(boy, 10)*

The forces of law and order not only constrain but protect. They are a necessary bulwark against destruction, holding back all the anonymous crowds who would otherwise be involved in violence. Such is children's view of human nature in the mass. Their generalization that 'everybody' would be violent might be an abstraction since it does not include themselves, but it is one which gives a clear view of the need for order in society. Without rules, they keep reiterating, there would be chaos, a chaos which would affect everyone.

'Half of us would be dead by now.'   *(boy, 10)*

This sense of human nature is not limited to the children's own country but is seen as universal. All over the world, children imply, there would be the same kind of outbreak of violence, individuals against each other, private, disorganized but destructive.

'They'd be going round the world and everybody would be beating up and people would be killed and knocked over.'   *(girl, 10)*

Violence, in terms of an unleashing of destructive energy, is disorganized. It is depicted as wilful and inevitable, private and without any particular motive apart from greed or hate. The violence is not directed against specific targets; the State itself is not a target for violence, but is only involved with it because it fights violence. Only occasionally is there a glimpse of violence being organized; then the forces of prevention are again the one barrier against what would be so much worse, as in the case of terrorists.

'The country and the world would be just terror, terror, be overrun by terrorists or whatever they are.' *(girl, 9)*

Here children's picture of the need to control people who would cause widespread destruction if they were given the chance is apt. They have been taught the importance of vigilance against murderous terrorists. They have grown up on the idea of deterrence; that if there were no threat of retaliation through nuclear weapons, countries would be overcome. They realize what would happen if there were no constraints over nations.

'Probably having a nuclear war by now.' *(girl, 11)*

It is just that children apply the same need for deterrence and control to all aspects of society, not just those in which armies have a place.

Children's sense of potential violence is based on their observation of what they know is happening in the present, even with all the forces of control intact. It seems obvious to them that things could be worse.

'There would be a lot more murdering than there is already. Even more.' *(girl, 10)*

Children accept that authority is a necessity, that the law needs to be weighty enough to prevent even worse outbreaks of violence than they already witness. They have a bleak, perhaps conservative, view of human nature. The universality of violent tendencies suggests that they accept that is how people are; not in one particular place or one particular time, but as a general rule. All over the world, they feel, there is a need for control or 'the world would just go bonkers', 'go crazy', 'be a mess'. This is because of the pleasure people are supposed to have in doing wrong.

'I think if we didn't have any police in the world it would be a bit of a mad one really. Well, there would be mucking around and everything really.' *(girl, 10)*

'Everyone would be doing the wrong thing.' *(girl, 11)*

Children accept both the tendency for people to do wrong and the sense that it is wrong. They retain their moral stance about misbehaviour whilst recognizing its universal existence.

'A lot more people might go around doing things they shouldn't.' *(girl, 9)*

'Everybody would be bad and people would get killed.' *(boy, 10)*

Children deplore people 'turning' bad as much as they deplore hooligans and rioters. Bad behaviour is not a new invention. It is always there and always needs constraining. For if there were no controls:

'People would just go around doing what they wanted to.' *(girl, 9)*

What people 'want to do' seems to need outer constraints rather than inner ones. It is as if children see a constant urge to go wild.

'Everybody would be doing what they like and then people, when they are let out, would be climbing on the walls and that.' *(boy, 9)*

It sounds as if the law were almost a physical constraint. The idea of unshackled freedom is not associated with pleasure, or with innocent pursuits. It is assumed that what people would eventually *want* to do would be to concentrate on stealing and destruction, or taking drugs.

'Everyone would be going round taking things . . . and there'd be houses being broken into and vandals all over the place.' *(boy, 11)*

'People would be shooting each other, taking things out of shops.' *(girl, 11)*

Children do not suggest that there would be strong inner restraints, or communal inhibitions that would prevent such an outbreak of illegality. They see the role of law as a strong counterpart to criminal activity, just as in the imagery given to the police in their confrontation of rioters. Behind the physical images of riot shields and baton charges lies the equally powerful but more abstract sense of force.

The law consists partly of prevention. This is the result of being in a world full of the symbols of violence, a violence that is rooted in human nature. The question remains why people should behave like this? What explanations are given of all that children witness, especially on the news? Occasionally they suggest that there are causes in addition to natural tendencies. Whilst it is difficult to grasp individual motives in hooliganism, children are aware of the dangers both of idleness and drink.

> 'I think some people behave badly when they get drunk. We've got one man in our village and he's always getting drunk. He bashes bottles over people's heads. Sometimes he can be very nice but sometimes not when he's drunk . . . put him in a mental health camp.' *(girl, 9)*

The solution to such a problem again implies that nothing can be done to reform or rehabilitate the man. For at the root of bad behaviour lies that fact that

> '. . . people just enjoy being bad.' *(girl, 10)*

Drink merely enhances this tendency, as does the opportunity afforded by having nothing better to do. A few children occasionally suggest that there are other reasons that lie behind bad behaviour, as much to do with the environment and upbringing as with desire.

> 'I think that they've either been brought up like that or they've got nothing to do and can't think of anything better to do.' *(girl, 9)*

> 'Sometimes it's not their fault. It's their parents' fault or friends who try to lead them on.' *(girl, 12)*

But these instances are rare.

Whatever the cause for bad behaviour, it is assumed that once set in certain ways, people will not change. Given certain circumstances, like football matches, or drink, people will exhibit more clearly their destructive tendencies. But they remain there, even if under restraint. Although the majority of children feel that it is inevitable that people will break the law, human nature being what it is, a few are reflective about the reasons for such actions. In addition to the feeling that 'they can't think of anything else to do' is the view that they 'had not been brought up properly', that some of the root causes lie in their home background, and environment.

The reasons given for such behaviour can be summed up in three short statements:

> '. . . because they are spoiled when they are young.' *(girl, 10)*

> '. . . because they can't help having something wrong with them-selves. They live in unpleasant houses.' *(boy, 10)*

> '. . . because they are not punished a lot when they are really bad.' *(girl, 12)*

Punishment has a central place in children's idea of the law. Once people are formed, and literally 'spoiled' by their environment, punishment becomes something other than fierce education. Children show no simple belief in natural goodness. They see that people can be made as well as born bad. But they do not think that people have much control over their own actions. A propensity to evil can be balanced by control. Children are unconvinced that people have much self-control. Control must therefore be externally applied. And punishment is a way of doing so; a deterrent and prevention rather than a means of reform. Persuasion and cajoling, or appealing to guilt rather than fear is not considered sensible, or effective.

> 'Because they just think it's stupid when they bring something up on television like. Quite a long time ago there's the . . . they've got to catch a murderer and "please don't do this" or "don't shoplift" and they're just going to think, "Oh, ha, ha," and go and do it. I just think they're not talking sense. They don't know what they're doing.' *(girl, 11)*

Strict rules are important, and these must be supported by equally strict deterrents. The threat of punishment is a necessity.

> 'People would just keep getting away with things; robbing banks and doing all the shops and things.' *(girl, 10)*

> 'If there were no laws and no punishment people would run around just killing people and robbing banks and there would be riots all the time and the police wouldn't be able to handle it.' *(boy, 10)*

The bleak view of human nature with its tendency to wickedness is matched by an equally hard view about the nature of punishment. The corollary to crime is the need for even harsher punishments, as a deterrent and as an inevitable response. Whilst children are aware that the majority of criminals are not caught, they feel that retribution should be harsher.

'I don't think murderers get it hard enough.'   *(girl, 11)*

'Some people get off lightly because there isn't any capital punishment.'   *(girl, 12)*

'People do not have proper prison sentences.'   *(boy, 12)*

Punishment is a necessary sanction in society, as in school. It is not seen as a means of teaching adults to behave differently but as a deterrent, for:

'If people do not get punished they keep doing bad things.'   *(girl, 10)*

Children are aware of the nature of punishment in their own lives, and do not dissociate themselves entirely with the tendency to behave badly. The images they cite might be far more extreme than anything they personally experience but, from an early age, they have a moral pragmatism that applies to themselves as well as others. They focus on the outcome of actions, and therefore punishment, rather than the motivation behind actions, but they do not expect people to feel good if they have harmed someone else.[2] And yet they witness what is clearly a deliberate attempt to pursue violence on the part of masses of people, as well as the crimes committed by individuals. It is difficult for them to associate their own experiences and all the examples of criminal behaviour given to them every day. But they do apply the same structure of rules and deterrents. And their pragmatism about other people also applies to themselves. Just as they are aware that people are not 'good' so they know that this is true of themselves.

'No, I'm not always good. I don't think one can be good all the time.'   *(boy, 12)*

They know not only their own limitations — 'playing about in class', 'bad temper', 'don't obey', 'keep leaving things lying about', 'people make me angry' — but some of the reasons for them. They know that they were easily provoked.

'If people annoy me, I get cross and do bad things.'   *(girl, 11)*

'Because I sometimes get temptated.'   *(girl, 10)*

But they also recognize that they could be naughty without provocation.

Whilst children are engaged in understanding the world in which they find themselves, they go through many processes of reassessment, of themselves and others. They see the evidence of human behaviour in its extreme forms on television. They are concerned about issues. They realize that the world is an unsafe place and accept that things are getting worse rather than better. They also know that they must make their own way, that they need protection from others and from themselves. So they believe in the possibilities of learning and the importance of upbringing and the necessity for punishment. As well as the good moments, the excitements and the pleasures of friendships, they are equally aware of the possibility of pain on a personal as well as a universal scale.

Whilst children perceive the consequences of upbringing and home environment and clearly compare the different circumstances in which people live, they also accept the arbitrariness of the world and the lack of any overriding order. They know that not all crime is punished and do not believe that sentencing is always just. They accept that the world is not perfect and that there are many dangers both personal and general. They do not always assume that they live in the best possible circumstances, and they doubt their own tendencies to be good, let alone that of other people. In their remarks, therefore, children show a subtle appreciation of their environment. They hold no sentimental views about themselves or about their circumstances. They exhibit, instead, a pragmatism that could possibly be a sounder basis for their understanding of the world than optimistic naïvety.

NOTES AND REFERENCES

1. Chukovsky, K. *From Two to Five*. Berkeley: University of California Press, 1963.
2. Nunner-Winkler, G., and Sodian, B. 'Children's understanding of moral emotions.' *Child Development* **59**(5), 1323–1338, 1988.

CHAPTER 10
Society in Sickness and in Health

'Well, there's things like murders and that. There's still a lot of them around. There's less than there could be.' *(girl, 9)*

The necessity of having strict laws and strong enforcement implies something about human nature. Children are not nurtured in the belief that people are naturally good, even from a early age. There might be a moral imperative that dictates that the world, as in story, contains the good and the bad. There might be a belief in each child that they *ought* to be good. But they do not have a sanguine view of human nature. Nor do they have a rosy view about society as a whole. Confronted as they are with evidence of violence and inequality, unhappiness and discontent, it would perhaps be surprising if children retained a happy view of society, both in their own country and elsewhere. Children accept the structure of a world divided between good and evil, and see society driven equally by the divisions between crime and the forces of law and order. They also see the two sides as less than completely distinct. The order of society is a fragile one, tense and in danger of collapse. In these circumstances children do not acquire an automatic belief in the rectitude of politicians or confidence in justice. Children's lack of optimism is more a lack of confidence.

When children analysed what they perceived of society as a whole, beyond the legal and political structures, the sense of what they had imbibed from the news again came across very strongly. Their lack of confidence led more than 80 per cent of them to a strongly expressed feeling that the world was becoming a more dangerous place to live, in terms of crime and in terms of war, and that violence was generally increasing. They hear their parents talk of higher levels of violence against children. They are no longer allowed to go out alone, whether in towns or woods. They are warned against strangers. And they hear reports of child abuse. Children create a framework of public events which seem to follow a pattern and in the context of which they need to understand their own lives. They are aware of what they see and read.

> 'I think people keep showing all the terrible things that have happened on the television and I think most families are looking at it and realizing how terrible it is but I don't think there is anything you can really do to stop it. The ordinary programmes have got all the divorced people and people going on and taking drinks and drugs.' *(girl, 10)*

It is a common reaction to the news to say how 'terrible' things are. Even at the centre of domestic life, with the family sharing an entertainment together, there is the unavoidable intrusion of bad news, of events that show people in the worst light. The fact that soap operas also deal with 'real' events serves both to highlight a vision of society, and to make the intrusion the more a part of everyday entertainment. One level of domestic worry is joined by reactions to public events:

> 'The budget is putting things up and people will keep on buying them. My Dad's getting more and more smokes. He's smoking all the time. I wish he would stop. He tells us his hands feel empty without a fag. I read the paper and there's so many crimes going on and murders and rapes.' *(boy, 8)*

One level of concern is associated naturally with another. The sense that things are 'getting worse' is not just an abstract feeling. It is one that is specifically linked to real events.

> 'Well, like in London, there are a lot of vandals in London and that . . . glue sniffers and things like that. I see things are getting worse because there's all sorts of bad things on the news. Only occasionally good things.' *(girl, 10)*

One of the results of television is the association of London with crime and violence.[1] Children who live in more rural areas no longer think of the excitement of large cities. They see, second-hand perhaps, all the signs of squalor and decay. And they know that the news concentrates on 'bad things' that take place in particular parts of the country.

> 'Some parts of the country are putting up more fighting than what was before and other people are being quiet and not mentioned on the news.' *(girl, 9)*

Children's awareness that the news concentrates on what is bad is a saving grace that enables them to keep things in perpective. It also helps them to see events that take place elsewhere in a balance with their own circumstances. There might be many criminal acts generally but these do not take place where they live. But, if any do, it makes an accumulated impact.

One of the results of all the bad news that they are given is the pervading sense that the world is getting worse. To some extent this is a universal and constant feeling in all generations. In young children it is marked by their own nostalgia for when they were infants and when they were unaware of the meanings of the images they saw. This sense of malaise is not just a general reaction to events — 'aren't things terrible nowadays?' — but a more clear perception about people. It is not 'things' but people who are getting worse.

'People are doing more bad things and they're more violent.'   *(girl, 9)*

Behind every riot children detect the individual. Behind the majesty of the law are the policemen. Politicians are not statesmen or heroes but individual people. Children do not just say there is 'more crime' in the abstract, but that there are more criminals.

'I think people are getting worse because people these days . . . I think people have been killing more. The riots are really bad.'   *(boy, 9)*

The answer to the spread of violence lies, as children reiterate, in more control.

'The violence is getting worse. We could get security forces to guard the areas where violence is always going on.'   *(boy, 7)*

There are means of limiting violence to certain places, places where there are 'gang wars'. The response is always to increase the manpower of security forces.

'Well, I think worse because of all this violence going on than it used to be . . . won't ever change . . . because if the police can't control the place it's going to get worse.'   *(boy, 10)*

The answer to the problem is to keep a firm lid on it.

But children's view of society is not all bleak. They expressly mention certain arrangements which indicate great improvements and which answer some of their own strictures, and fears. Children's sense of the need for greater police powers and more control of crime is sometimes seen to be met.

'The way they are stopping people from doing things.' *(girl, 10)*

Improvement is seen to lie in the greater sophistication shown by the police in controlling riots or hooligans:

'All the equipment's getting better. The police can control riots better.' *(girl, 10)*

It is seen to be due to the police that there's 'not so much killing and stealing' rather than to any change in society as a whole, let alone in human nature. Children observe the need for strict enforcement of the law.

'Things are being stopped. Sort of drinking, driving and things like that which the police stop and everything.' *(girl, 11)*

'Well, drunk drivers are not allowed to drive around without being checked on, are they? Laws are clamping down.' *(girl, 11)*

The close association of laws with enforcement is seen in the way children suggest that the creation of new laws — 'the way the country handles things' — brings about changes in behaviour.

'They're making some new laws up that they should have made up a long time ago.' *(girl, 8)*

It is as if part of the blame for disorder lay in not anticipating and controlling people. Given the propensity for football fans to behave in certain ways, the answer lies in finding sensible means of prevention. Children suggest that there is always a need for new laws — always stricter ones. Nevertheless, there are indications of the awareness that even if there are laws, people will not necessarily obey them. The need for stricter enforcement is constantly reiterated even if they can cause peculiar reactions.

'The laws are becoming more horrible. That's the only thing that's changing.' *(girl, 7)*

One indication that the world is becoming a better place to live in lies in the greater sophistication of police control. This is partly due to the improvement of their equipment. Children are aware of the potential of technology generally and indicate computers in particular as a sign of positive change.

'Well, they've got lots of new things like computers. Technology's improving.' *(girl, 10)*

'I think they're getting a tiny weeny little bit better. There's more sort of . . . more buildings and factories and more technology and computer technology. You can do a lot more things now by just touching a few keys on a keyboard. They'll build houses next with a keyboard.' *(boy, 9)*

The idea of technology is not an abstract one. Children often link the power of computers with robotics, with palpable results. They see that technological advances lead to the building of more houses, and to the building of 'new ideas like the Channel Tunnel'. And then there are other new creations to enhance the world.

'They way they are building the tunnel. And the new Disney thing in France. I think that's a good idea.' *(girl, 9)*

Thus not all is gloom. One child also notices another change, thanks to the enforcement of new legislation.

'Strikes . . . we're not having so many of them.' *(boy, 9)*

Not all is gloom, and yet the majority of children only see things getting worse. Where there is improvement it lies in technology and control, not in any fundamental or even slight change in society. Even the realization of changes in laws governing strikes and pickets is hedged with equivocation.

'Well, people are bombing and they don't get caught. Some of them get away. Things like pickets, they're getting better because they're going back and the things that are getting worse is some of the things Margaret Thatcher's doing.' *(boy, 8)*

Children's statements about the need for more police powers in the prevention of crime, for stricter laws more strictly enforced, arises from the pervasive feeling that the world is becoming an unsafe place. They hear about rape and murder almost every day. And they start to lose confidence in their ability to do what they want to.

'You can hardly go out and walk the streets like people say you used to because there's so many things going on.' *(girl, 11)*

Children become accustomed to hearing the present contrasted with the past. This fosters the sense that things are getting worse, that the decline in social behaviour will continue, and violent crime grow steadily worse. Those who argue that people have always behaved as badly as at the present time cannot argue against the fact that today more people *know* about these things. Rumour and anecdote have always been powerful means of learning news, but there can never have been such a number of crimes disseminated into people's consciousness every day.

Children are strongly aware of the rise of sexual crimes, 'like people raping'.

'I think they are getting worse because . . . there's people who go around mugging old ladies and rapes and things like that.' *(girl, 11)*

'Definitely worse. I've forgotten where it was but there are all sorts of robberies and rape and things like that.' *(boy, 10)*

Even before children are aware of the implications, they are aware of the acts. They hear examples, with details of evidence, of a range of violent sexual acts.

'Now girls cannot go out in case there's a man waiting for them. There's so many people getting raped.' *(girl, 12)*

'The world could be a better place if there wasn't so much sexual violence.' *(boy, 11)*

The prevalence of violence in different forms strikes children as the most obvious sign of decline. Some of them feel personally inhibited and threatened by violence; all of them suggest that violence is becoming more common, more everyday. Sexual violence is only one example. Many cite murders.

'Murder and that because there's more murders now than there was.' *(boy, 11)*

'Nothing can be done to stop them. Murders are getting worse.' *(boy, 9)*

'People are getting murdered everywhere.' *(girl, 9)*

Old people are thought to be particularly vulnerable to attack.

Although children extrapolate their fear of violence from a mass of details, and particular cases, such details accumulate into a more generalizable feeling. They have a general, but not abstract, sense

137

of the rise of violence, perceived to include large numbers of people. At the heart of their concern lie their fear of riots — violence in a public form, violence which includes masses of people. The increase in the number of murders involves fear of individuals; each act is notorious. But riots seem like outbreaks of a collective kind that involve many people, and potentially, all.

> 'It's changing for the worse really because football players are being hit by bottles and things and there's been lots of riots and things going on.' *(girl, 11)*

> 'Well, they used to get better but now they're getting worse. There are more riots now. There are more murders. There are more rapes and other things like that.' *(boy, 11)*

Of all the instances of social disorder it is visions of rioting that most strike children. This is what they particularly cite to demonstrate that things are getting worse, that there used not to be such things.

> 'Worse. There's more riots and that, and at football matches people just throw smoke bombs all over the place.' *(boy, 10)*

> 'Well, there never really used to be fights like riots and that sort of thing.' *(girl, 11)*

The images are of a society out of control:

> 'I think it's disgraceful.' *(boy, 10)*

But signs of disorder are not just public ones, and not only matters of violence. There are many other symbols of despair that children cite in support of their contention. They are aware of what they see as an increase in diseases and in drugs. It is interesting to note how they tend to link the two.

> 'Well there's the fear of AIDS, which isn't all that big at the moment. There's the drugs, which is bad, and I'm never going to take any. I never want to. Sometimes I've had an idea that people might smuggle drugs. They could smuggle drugs in packets of glucose because glucose looks like cocaine. I was a bit put off by that.' *(boy, 10)*

Detailed knowledge is balanced by distaste. But, whatever the personal opinion, the awareness is there, together with the awareness that there seem to be an ever-increasing number of additional dangers. The abuse of drugs is known to be a comparatively recent phenomena; AIDS is even more recent. The sense of 'things getting worse' is based on more than a general instinct.

'Riots and drugs, smoking, and people dying of cancer and all that. It just gets worse and worse. It can't be helped.' *(boy, 10)*

The abuse of drugs again affects a large number of ordinary people, not just a few professional criminals who are making money out of their international operations. Like a disease, the taking of drugs spreads. Like smoking tobacco it is seen as an unpleasant habit, as well as illegal.

'Heroin and the young people smoking . . . because people aren't obeying the law.' *(girl, 11)*

The taking of drugs is not seen by children as a symptom of some kind of previous failure, or despair. But it is seen as possible cause for further crime, as drink is. Drugs are seen as part of the general malaise.

'Well, people keep going on about all the pay rises and things. All the violence is getting worse. Well, some of them take drugs just to be the same as other people and to sort of keep in touch with what everyone is doing, and some people have heard somebody insult them in some sort of way and they take it out on everything.' *(girl, 10)*

Pictures of people taking drugs, meant as warnings, are also evidence. More evidence comes from the misuse of drink. We have already noted how drinking is one element in the football hooligan's armour. But it has a more widespread effect, in children's eyes.

'Lots of people are getting drunk and the policemen are after them. And policemen get killed by lots of bad people.' *(girl, 8)*

'Like drinking's getting worse. Murders are getting worse and things like that.' *(girl, 10)*

Drugs and drink are cited as symptoms of decay. But there is also recognition of other factors that cause misery.

'They are getting worse because all the prices of food is going up and people, if they can't afford it, they can't live.' *(boy, 10)*

Poverty, as well as unemployment, is seen as an important factor. For some it's a matter of not being able to afford luxuries, a matter of inflation.

'All the money for things are going up and all that. Petrol and things like that.' *(boy, 10)*

For others, the lack of money is seen not as being part of a general decline — or 'the pound against the American dollar' but a lack which has a palpable effect:

'Some things are getting worse. More people having to live in council houses.' *(girl, 9)*

Children's sense of insecurity in their society is supported by many instances of social decay, from poverty, and disease, to outbreaks of individual or collective violence. But their sense of insecurity also has a global context. The threat of nuclear war still remains part of their consciousness. Whilst children understand deterrence in terms of sanctions, and threats of punishments, they are also conscious of the possibility of nuclear wars.

'Bombs, because it kills millions of people.' *(boy, 10)*

'The worst thing that could happen is for everyone to die, except me.' *(girl, 11)*

But children are also aware of the many conventional wars that take place.

'I think that going to the war sometimes, 'cos of nuclear missiles and that and everyone going on the rampage and the blacks in other countries.' *(boy, 11)*

'Well, if you clear up one war then another one's bound to start because they're not happy at the way you cleared up the other war.' *(girl, 11)*

Children's sense of international affairs tends to centre on two matters; war and starvation. With war their great fear is of nuclear weapons. Starvation they nearly always associate with Africa, especially Ethiopia.

'Well, some things are getting better, some things are getting worse. Well, war and threats are getting worse, you know, when the bombs and things, nuclear missiles and things, but some things are getting better. Helping people in Ethiopia, you know: we're thinking of them more than just leaving them.' *(girl, 10)*

When evidence of war and bombs is wanting, the IRA provide it:

'The IRA are doing a few more attacks. I don't really know about how things have gone wrong. I just think it's getting worse.' *(boy, 9)*

There is always evidence of trouble in some parts of the world. The name of the country might change, but there is always news of war, of starvation, or efforts to bring aid. There are always television pictures of people fighting and natural disasters. Some places, like Northern Ireland, are so permanently in the news that they are no longer spectacular. For children the general impression is that the human condition is one of almost universal discontent and suffering. They know from their own domestic experience that day-to-day life is peaceful. But they are not presented with pictures of day-to-day life elsewhere. They hear instead of civil wars and revolutions, of riots and camps for the starving. The issue then is more than a matter of local political difficulty. And even beyond the international context lie even more permanent and long-term issues of which children are aware. They contrast environmental issues with the technological advances of building more houses.

'Getting better in technology and things . . . but some things are not getting any gooder. People are killing more and more animals and chopping down more and more trees and building more and more towns and houses. Some people just don't care.' *(boy, 10)*

'Things are getting worse really with people chopping down trees in wildlife environments and building houses. I don't think that's very good because we've got enough houses and office blocks and you know it's just being cruel to animals and, in a way, throwing your money away.' *(boy, 11)*

Children's sympathy for 'green' issues contrasts with their mixed feelings about housing. They are concerned that people *should* be housed, and admire the technological achievement of office blocks and houses. And yet they see that kind of advance appearing at the expense of the environment. Just as advances in technology can lead to the loss of jobs, so 'housing facilities' spell the destruction of trees and animals.

Children are sensitive to their surroundings. Environmental issues are not global abstractions but affect where children live. That is why they have such equivocal feelings about housing developments. That is also why they see litter as another example of general decay.

'If all the people that drop their litter and make it all nasty and horrible I would say it's not getting any better.' *(boy, 9)*

They can be critical and objective about the places in which they live, and can contrast their own environment with other potential places to live. They have been on holiday or seen on television places of great visual attraction.

'I wish I lived in a cottage with roses growing up the wall, with a pretty little garden.' *(girl, 11)*

But it does not need a cosy image to lead children to be objective about their own towns.

'. . . because where I live is so untidy, boring and doesn't look pleasant.' *(girl, 12)*

Children might find the place where they live 'boring' but they have to accept it as the place in which they have their home and their friends. Never are their own circumstances seen in complete contrast to other places. When they see what happens on the news they don't dismiss it as something that could only happen in a distant country.

Children's concern with the future arises from their concern with their own circumstances. The age of optimism seems long past. Whilst children acknowledge technical progress, they do not present any belief in people improving, whatever is done about their conditions and upbringing. Human progress, they suggest, depends on the enforcement of stricter laws, on containing criminal tendencies. They fear that people will generally become worse behaved, less obedient to the law.

'If the government says one thing and they don't agree with it, they start rioting and things like that.' *(girl, 10)*

Given the wilfulness of human nature there are two choices: either to:

'Just leave it alone and let them sort it out between them.' *(girl, 10)*

or to prevent any outbreaks by stricter control. It is the latter that children feel is necessary. Their vision of the future includes not only 'being shot and there's too much crime and things', but the need to respond in kind. They see the police being armed.

'There's riots and there's the guns that people have to wear. The police are going to have to wear guns at airports.' *(girl, 11)*

Children's sense that the 'world is getting worse' is supported by a whole range of examples that they give. They can present crime figures, the rise in the number of burglaries, rapes and murders committed, and the decline in the percentages of detections. They can cite the numbers of wars and the international scale of a series of disasters of one kind or another. And they perceive examples of mayhem presented on television so that the statistics are clothed with clear images:

'Rioting and all the killing going on, and everything: all the burglaries. It's really bad.' *(girl, 10)*

In this sense of decay all kinds of material becomes pressed together including accidents and the education system. It is as if there were so many examples of what is wrong that any sense of advance is infused by predictions of despair. If the good things are technological, and the bad things are the realities of human nature, the only answer lies in the greater powers of control.

'They're getting worse. There's nuclear missiles. There's riots and there's the guns . . . I think they are getting worse because there's people who go around mugging old ladies and rapes and things like that. I think it is going to stop suddenly, I think. Because there'll be a sudden law and it'll all stop, like in a war they'd most probably have a curfew.' *(girl, 11)*

NOTES AND REFERENCES

1. *Thatcher's Children. What 16–18 Year Olds Want from Their Working Lives.* Wilton, Wilts: Stapleford Partnerships, 1990.

CHAPTER 11
Conclusions

'They take them to a place where they're disciplined and made to obey and not break the law.' *(boy, 10)*

The two major studies of what makes primary and secondary schools effective come to very similar conclusions.[1] They dispel the myth that it depends on extraneous factors, like home background. Instead they draw up a list of items which show that schools with similar profiles in terms of buildings and income differ from each other markedly in terms of pupil motivation and success. At the heart of the school lies the question of 'ethos'. This is not easy to define.[2] It depends on attitudes, on a common sense of purpose, and on teachers' shared beliefs and interrelationships. It might seem an abstract concept but mood and tone is powerful and pervasive.

Schools, like the people in them, are strongly governed by atmosphere. The tone of a school, positive or negative, optimistic or careless, is felt as an almost palpable thing. It affects the ways in which pupils approach their work; it underpins or undermines discipline; it makes special events satisfying rather than a cause of difficulty; and it enhances or distracts from teachers' presentations of the curriculum. Each individual in the school contributes to, and shares, the collective mood.

If ethos is important in the small society of a school it is also important in society as a whole. Shared expectations and general atmospheres are deeply effective in bringing about success or failure. Nothing could seem more distant from emotional climates than the monolithic financial markets, with investments and deals seemingly dependent on hard-headed pragmatism. And yet nothing could be more affected by mood than shares. A recession is a collective sharing of despondency: every fall or rise in the stock market is governed by pessimism or optimism. There might be excuses for the mood, a rationale that suggests that people are anticipating events, and collecting a series of gnomic signs. But in the end it is a general atmosphere that sways financial markets, that drives a country into expansion or recession.

Governments are also governed by mood and tone. From the 'Winter of Discontent' to the particular manifestations of Thatcherism, the government both reflects and imposes a mood. A government presents itself not so much in terms of clear policy statements but in terms of pervasive attitudes. What it does is not always as important as the way it goes about doing it:

> The last temptation is the greatest treason;
> To do the right thing for the wrong reason.
>
> T. S. Eliot, *Murder in the Cathedral*

An elected government is a clear indication of a shared mood which affects all engaged in education. Much has been made of the feelings of teachers, of their sense of being undermined and undervalued, because morale affects not only teacher supply but the way in which teachers perform in the classroom. The ethos of the school therefore is not just contained within the confines of a particular space but is affected by the community and the society it is in. The same tone which manifests itself in other social institutions is reflected in schools.

One of the most pervasive attitudes in the last few years is expressed in the idea of competition. This can have a hard edge. In the German language it is possible to make a distinction between kindly competition and hard competition.[3] Recently in Great Britain, and elsewhere, the two seem to have become inseparable. The freedom of privatization is linked to the threat of accountability. Measurement of success is also revelation of failure. Performance indicators are set up to demonstrate all that is wrong. Increasing numbers of appraisers and inspectors are added to ensure the given criteria are complied with. And all this accountability derives from the essential belief that people cannot be trusted to do a good job. The power of market forces in improving competition might be a very important political idea, but it is linked closely with the sense that some are going to fail, that all is not well with society and that people need to be made more accountable for their actions.

Those who visit more than one school will know how important such pervasive attitudes are: not just in terms of stress but in the way in which people go about their daily business. The role of the headteacher is changed from academic leader to financial controller. The class teacher is no longer in control of the curriculum, but delivers it against set targets. Schools are therefore clearly affected by changes in mood as well as policy. But schools are only one example of the shifts in emphasis that affect all parts of society.

Children are very susceptible to mood. At a superficial level we see this demonstrated in their collective reactions to the weather. But they are also more deeply affected by the attitudes of society. At the heart of children's analysis of society lies a shared mood. This collective consciousness is a long way distant from the naïve optimism with which childhood is often associated. Children are, after all, just as influenced by the society of which they are part as other people. They also feel the assumptions that underlie the stress on competition. They both acknowledge the impact that it has on them and see the difference it makes to adults, to parents and relations as well as teachers. And while they might not be interested in the particular arguments that are put forward by politicians they do understand the tone in which they are said.

Children reflect a society which seems to have lost its optimism and self-belief. Whilst they realistically acknowledge cases of advance, mostly technical, they do not suggest optimism for the future. They have been listening, like others, not only to years of disasters, wars and threats of wars, trouble with criminals and crowds, but have heard politicians making it quite clear that these are due to human folly. An accident is followed by blame; the inquiry is set up to find someone to punish. But it also seems the everyday duty of democratic politics to cast doubt on people's integrity.

Children demonstrate that they have little belief in the perfectibility of human nature. In this respect they are very conservative. They witness too many examples of natural depravity to believe that society will improve. They know that they can complain about what happens but they recognize that complaints will make little or no difference. They see the powerful arguments for competition, for distinctions between people, for choice, and know that they must look after themselves. They are aware of the larger future into which they will enter. They do not see schools as being separated from their own advance, as understood in terms of employment.[4] Children therefore digest the mood that affects teachers, stockbrokers and all in society who have access to the presentations of newspapers and television.

Mood is especially important for children because of the ways in which they view television and overhear remarks. Like many adults, children do not analyse all they see. They do not understand the details. They are not encouraged to scrutinize the news or share their vision of the world. Their approach to television as a medium of entertainment means that they view it superficially. A series of images and statements cohere into a very general blur. Just as adults find it difficult to recall the items of news they heard on the radio in the morning, so children find it difficult to pick out particular items. But they do detect the tone.

Children also learn to interpret what they hear in their own way. There is no framework of understanding into which their reflections can be placed. It is as if children's education were dominated by the overheard remark.[5] They listen in to other people's opinions. They watch their parents' laconic reactions. And they share these reactions with each other. It is not as if they see the adult world as separate and of no interest to them. On the contrary, they show such interest that they struggle hard to make sense of it in their own way. But they are not helped or encouraged. In the absence of analysis, tone is crucial.

Since schools are amongst the first organizations that children experience they link the way they run with the way that society is run. And they have plenty of time to analyse. They see the given assumptions, the centres of power, the sometimes arbitrary decisions. They are aware of the difference in tone between one classroom and another. They know where they like to work and where the peer group pressure forces them not to. And they subconsciously connect the attitudes of their parents to details of their behaviour and the shared ethos of a collection of adults. At the same time, children overhear the opinions of those who are in charge of the law, or the police, or football stadia, and they imbibe opinions about other countries.

From the point of view of the child, society is presented in a series of confused images. The essential tenets of behaviour are learned from parents and other close adults. But private standards of morality are developed in a context which is larger; where different

147

people have different standards, where it is possible to behave in certain ways in one place but not another. Just as the mistakes children make are often a matter of confusion, of inappropriate behaviour, so they see a range of types of people and reactions that do not present a standard or consistent moral tone. Nothing could be more varied than the approaches of television presenters, from those that 'front' popular music shows for young children, to news readers. Society cannot be seen as a monolithic whole but as a confusion of attitudes. And children must make sense of it all.

Schools do little to ease the confusion. It might seem at first that the school is a haven of order. Schools might not explain anything about society, but they appear to demonstrate the way society works. In fact, for the individual child, school is not felt as a complete autonomy. The ethos of a school is not presented as a series of firm social values. The morality of individual behaviour is stressed — how not to disrupt others, how to obey teachers — but children also see many of the ambiguities, moments when rules are imposed and others where they are not. Much has been made of the hegemony of the school, imposing conservative attitudes on people.[6] Many of these attitudes are, however, generally held by many people and reflected by the school. When children seek to test out how firm the school's commitment to discipline is, they are reflecting a more widespread testing of society. The connection between the 'joker' in the class, finding out whether it is possible to undermine the authority of the teacher, and the attitudes of an individual to the law, is a close one.[7] Children understand the ambivalence of their parents' feelings about some rules, and also witness the classic impositions of law in popular television series and films. Schools cannot be separated from the society they are in, even if they seemingly ignore it.

The school is connected closely with its environment and shares many of the same problems. Every day the children come into school they understand the context in which it is placed. They see policemen; they see the control of transport; they notice the litter; they go past decaying buildings. Whilst schools look different from other buildings they are also affected by the need of management and control, and reflect the same lack of resources or the visual decay of the environments in which they are placed. The same visual disparities of billboards, signs and notices are seen within and outside school.

But children are also given evidence of society in a whole variety of individual cases. On the one hand, they see how society organizes itself to deal with collective problems, such as transport and waste disposal. On the other hand, they see beggars and tramps who are clearly escaping the ordering of society. And they also hear and see all the signs of emergencies, of something going wrong, whether an accident or crime. Their world is not usually that of rural quiet, but inescapably the world of movement, and sound: all the signs and sirens of collective and official organization. And their personal experience is bolstered by the same scenes depicted on television or in the newspapers. Thus the evidence that children need to gain a coherent sense of society is presented to them piecemeal. First they see the images; only years later are they presented with the concepts and the reasons.

When children see glimpses of social organization on the streets, these inevitably include major contrasts in wealth and status. Whatever vision there might be of a classless society and of equality for all, children are presented with a series of pictures that celebrate differences. The very wealthy are featured in all their glory; the powerful are interviewed. The results of fame are kept constantly before the televison audiences and the adulation of pop stars is encouraged. At the same time the homeless and the very poor are made into articles and programmes. One of the first most powerful concepts that children receive is about the unequal distribution of wealth. The tone of competitiveness is manifested in the imagery of the very poor. However much such contrasts are deplored, they are nevertheless part of children's early consciousness. It is not only the starving populations of parts of Africa that are brought to children's attention but the urban poor much closer to home.

Whilst children witness signs of poverty, they also learn that there is nothing that they can do about it. They are in no position to change things. They are aware of the place of the State in the collection of taxes, and know about social security benefits. But the support of the very poor is not seen as a personal responsibility. How can it be? Children are made aware of the possibilities of charity every time they are involved in taking collections, or putting on an evening performance. But the poor are always with them.

The needs of those more unfortunate than themselves are contrasted with the images of fame and wealth. The concern with one is often juxtaposed with the celebration of the other in the same magazine or programme. Advertisements underline the prestige afforded by ownership. Given children's susceptibility to snobbery and self-consciousness, such contrasts of status have a strong potency. Children can be easily embarrassed by the way they perceive their parents behaving inappropriately. They can also become conscious of their parents' status in terms of possessions. After all, distinctions to be made between rich and poor cars are not only the stuff of magazines but, in terms of how old a car is, a matter of government advertising through registration numbers.

Society is closely observed in all its contrasts. Children learn to 'know their place' as well as see how powerful some people can be. Children sense that there is a cabal of powerful individuals who 'know the right person', a group from which children and their families are excluded. The sense that different people possess sharply differentiated amounts of power is underlined by the fact that there is little anonymity from the public gaze, whether the person is a popular entertainer or appears in the business pages. Children have a natural respect for the achievements of their own parents, for instance:

> 'I'd like to be a scientist and doctor and work for my Dad . . . He works on body scanners. He's not a doctor but he makes the big magnets which make the body scanner . . . He's one of the brainiest. Everyone has to ring him up because they're usually getting stuck . . .'
> *(boy, 10)*

But he also points out that his father is not a 'big decision-maker' compared to Mrs Thatcher, only a 'small' one.

Children are aware of the status of their parents and of the power of the Prime Minister, as well as the influence of those who advise him. They are taught about the hierarchies of society, not just the contrasts between rich and poor. Personal self-consciousness is embedded in the imagery of possessions. The question then is how early they learn to be jealous, or to feel superior. Before they develop a sophisticated sense of their own place in society, children learn to view society as disparate and yet unchanging. They observe the varieties of systems of control. They fear the masses who might get out of order; they respect the need for the repression of those who break the law. And they do this more with the sense of necessity than with any firm belief in the morality of good against evil.

Children know that they will have to fit into the society they see so vividly portrayed on television. They know that they will need to win jobs and this itself gives an underlying purpose to schools, even if it is one that is not discussed. Their views of the jobs that they are likely to get is on the whole realistic. Having seen teachers and nurses in action they can imagine filling posts of that kind. But they are much more influenced by the example of their parents, especially if their parent's post has a professional aspect. At the same time there is an element of fantasy that they willingly allow themselves when they say that they would like to be a veterinary surgeon or a show-jumper. Whilst children of 5 might have a fairly hazy idea of what a job is — 'I'd like to be a poet' — they are already aware that they will need to get one, for unemployment is a recognized disaster. Society is not assumed to give everyone jobs, but the general vision of society as a whole is closely associated with work, with all the functions that people carry out. The recognition of the importance of firemen or policemen adds to the sense of society as providing necessary jobs. The leisure industry is barely mentioned in terms of normal jobs. To be paid as an entertainer is not perceived as a realistic option.

Children develop realistic attitudes towards the world of work, even in the absence of detailed analysis of the underlying social base. They know about the worlds of industry, often from their peers and their parents. One of the reasons for such understanding is because children structure their knowledge through talking to each other. The importance of the overheard remark has already been mentioned. Its potency comes about because it usually consists of two people talking about a third. It suggests all the authority of anonymity, like a rumour.[8] One of the prime places in which two people share opinions about a third is in front of the television. Not much conversation takes place in terms of lengthy analysis, but reactions and opinions are both individual and shared. The extent to which parents use television to talk about issues varies, but very few use it as a starting point for conversation. Some try to control reactions; the majority are distinctly *laissez-faire*.[9] Nevertheless, basic reactions of disgust or pleasure, of despair or satisfaction are associated with what television presents.

151

Children acquire strongly felt opinions from their shared observation of television. They also bolster each other's opinions. We know that by the time babies are 7 to 8 months old they are tuned to different emotional expressions of adults. They do not suddenly discard this ability. Indeed they develop it, only learning to be less obvious in the expression of their reactions. And children also learn a whole range of social abilities from a very young age.[10] They argue with their parents and are interested in transgressing rules. In their second year children understand others' goals and social rules. They co-operate in play, co-ordinate actions, and comfort each other. They are very quick to detect moods and understand other people's points of view.

> 'As witnesses to arguments between their siblings and mothers the children show a sensitivity to both the topic of the dispute and the interests of the antagonists.'[11]

If this it true of infants, what then of children aged 6 and beyond?

The natural ability to see other people's points of view comes through the experience of negotiating with them, from knowing their *own* points of view. And yet this ability is not developed in a formal way. Although the concept of empathy is discussed in some areas of the curriculum it seems to be an afterthought rather than a central discipline. Children are quick to learn *how* people think but are rarely taught *what* they think and why. And so, in their games, children learn from each other. They relate anecdotes from their experience. They connect ideas to what they have observed on the public media. And they construct a sense of the world into which new items of information must fit.

The fact that children do not acquire formal knowledge of the judicial system or the rationale of the constitution does not mean that they are ignorant but that they might gain a distorted view, or one which finds some details more important than others. Politicians, for example, have a clear opinion about how they present themselves. They believe that to have all that they say recorded is perfect bliss. They accuse the media of bias if they are not quoted in full, or worse still, not quoted at all. Politicians seem to believe in the persuasive power of their own words, as if there were a whole world waiting with bated breath for their wisdom. They appear to be driven by a belief in propaganda. But the audience takes in quite different messages. They only pay close attention to what a politician says if they already agree.[12] What the audience retains, instead, is a bias against or for the speaker, whatever he or she is saying.

Children are supposed to take in information from the media however half-hearted their attention. But the messages that they receive are on a different level. They are not limited to the verbal and rational. They are more to do with general attitudes. An audience learning French, for example, should be expected to have acquired a larger vocabulary when being tested after the end of an educational television series. But they might just as well have learned a bias against France.[13] So children learn prejudices about politicians, generally only half believing what they say. Indeed, given that politicians talk so much, they are amongst the least popular aspects of television. Allied to a distaste for talking heads, children acquire a picture of political behaviour which is at a very different level from reasoned argument. They see the waving of papers, hear the shouts of, 'Order, order', and observe the ritual abuse of the House of Commons. And they are also fed a series of photo-opportunities, when politicians and others put on peculiar costumes for the sake of an interesting picture.

The different kinds of presentation of larger political ideas are not simply the mixture of fact and fantasy. Indeed, the imagery of debate, party conferences and wild behaviour in Parliament is far more concrete than the abstract idea. The politician stops talking, but the image lingers on. The visual imagery of the State is conveyed more easily than its meaning: the pomp and ceremony of the legal system is balanced by pictures of rioting prisoners; the rows of riot police are confronted by the shouting masses. This imagery is powerful.

The images of mass society are also indubitably real. When children create their idiosyncratic views of the world they do not do so by mixing up fact with fantasy. From an early age they are well aware of the difference. To take one example, children are exposed to many fantasized detectives on television, both English and American. These are depicted as heroes in one way or another: heroes of action or the more laconic anti-heroes of reflection. Both types prevail, despite all opposition and difficulties. Children are completely aware of the differences between these portrayals and the actual, routine, role of policemen.[14] When children talk about the police they give no hint of the fantasy elements of television. The pictures they present come from the news. And whilst children would quite like the idea of acting as a policeman in a television series — for that means fame and money — they do not like the thought of joining the real police force. They know the reality to be boring as well as dangerous.

When children take on the imagery of television, with the stress on headlines and news that lends itself to pictures, they are presented with a distorted sense of reality. Given their awareness of the distinction between truth and fantasy, can they also detect the distortion? The problem for children is that what they are presented with is real, and it is presented without conceptual explanation. Children have to make sense of what they see in their own terms, long before anyone helps them to analyse it. The world of the news, which describes society, highlights certain kinds of activity to which the audience is a passive spectator. So children learn to accept what they see as all part of a system.

Society is presented to children in simplified terms. People are bad. They are caught and punished by other people whose job is to punish them. People don't change, because there are new examples of crime everyday. The pragmatic, sometimes harsh views expressed by children derive from the ways in which they connect the evidence given to them. Power lies in the hands of the Prime Minister. Society has clear means of controlling violence. It raises money by taxation. At the same time children have developed the underlying idea that each person must look after himself, and that there is little that can be done.

When society is presented in simple imagery it looks monolithic. Personal experience from children's points of view, after all, remains private; but outside the small circle of friends and acquaintances appear anonymous crowds. Children are not taught about their place in society. They are aware of the idea of voting but do not know what it entails. They know that they can protest, but do not know about Citizens Advice Bureaux. They realize that other people can influence what happens but are ignorant of their own rights.

Some would argue that children are ignorant of their place in society because they have no rights. Certainly children's place is an uneasy one because there is no rite of passage into adulthood. They see all that adults see, as if there were nothing hidden from them.[15] But the adults do not talk about it. Children are neither initiated into adulthood, nor kept within the 'ignorance' of childhood. They observe until the time when they are suddenly responsible for their own actions. The age of consent and the age of voting are reduced; but little attention is paid to preparing for the responsibility.

In the stories that children are encouraged to read, and which they use to make sense of the world, there are profound themes. Literature addresses the central issues: the idea of the self, the struggle between good and evil, and the understanding of others. These are also the themes of society. But in stories there are conclusions. They make sense. The images that children receive on the news are rarely finished. They are glimpses into a long-running saga; both one-off incidents, and a complex whole. And the way they are presented is assertive, without description and with little explanation of the context. Thus children hear of significant events.

Some of the ways in which society is presented is reflected in children's reactions. Children generally learn to enjoy the accumulation of facts before they acquire the taste for asserting moralities.[16] But children are encouraged to assert preferences for pop stars or football clubs in magazines and television shows. Such assertions of favouritism implies a knowledge of alternatives but seems to be given without explanation or justification. This assertiveness is partly a matter of tone. 'I know what I like.' It is also using the norms of a shared social phenomenon to make an individual taste. But the assertion of a fan is the stronger because such favouritism does not suggest real individuality. 'My favourite colour is yellow' might seem to assert a personal taste, but is also a sign of connection with a social group. Assertions are signs of collective identity rather than individuality.

Children acquire information through the assertions of the news. One piece of information follows another in a seemingly random order. Only occasionally, as in a war or preparation for war, is there a connection between one bulletin and another over a matter of days. Otherwise the world is presented as a place where things might erupt at any time. Such presentations bolster the belief that the world would be out of control if such explosive forces were not repressed. The emphasis of the news is partly on extraordinary

155

events, for the news presenters seek excitement and need to feed off violent images, and partly on the reaction to these events.[17]

Children reflect such presentations with a belief in the need to control. The emphasis is on discipline rather than cure, as if it were entirely natural that some people would behave badly. But children are not the only ones who accept the view that it is the responsibility of those who are concerned with law and order to control and suppress crime. Government ministers pronounce that a rise in the crime rate is due to the lack of crime prevention by ordinary citizens, who should do more to protect their property. It is as if they pity the poor innocent criminal tempted beyond reason by the wicked victim. Such an acceptance of criminality is echoed in the acceptance of the need for discipline in schools. There, as government reports suggest, the problem of violence in schools must be overcome by greater control by teachers.[18]

The sense of natural human depravity which society needs to control is a pervasive one, not just invented by children. They are taught early to observe the worst forms of human behaviour, and to form the view that people are naturally bad, some in small ways and some in ways that are wholly unacceptable. But children also grow into the belief that people are unreformable. Bad behaviour warrants the threat of punishment as the only effective deterrent. Pictures on the news gradually congeal into a general social system.

'Well, I was watching the news yesterday and they said that a lady had been punched by a policeman and I think sometimes they go a bit far by handling the people when they're rioting. But they have to be quite rough otherwise they're not going to get anywhere.' *(girl, 10)*

The police have to be 'quite rough' because they reflect the violence of the general public. The same girl goes on:

'And the local kids who tend to be riotous . . . I think they're local kids . . . they chuck things at them and they use all the normal equipment and some of the head policemen, they have plastic shields and one of the head policemen throws a petrol bomb at them. If one of the boys did it, they'd probably lose their confidence with it.'

Given the imagery of television, the possible confusion is telling.

If control is seen as necessary, it implies that some people need the power to wield it. Children have a fairly vague idea of the actual functions of a president or prime minister, but they are certain of their authority. But the most clear examples of power are not abstract ideas but the ability to respond to violence with definite actions. The constitution is visible in the decisions that governments make and in the symbols of power — law courts, prisons and the police. The visible symbols of the State become the framework of children's understanding. The more abstract concepts of society are formed later, through interpretation of the more obvious manifestations of social order and disorder. Children assume that the use of force is a crucial requisite of the State. Society is only kept in a semblance of order by the forces of law and order.

Children very rarely mention the possibility of redemption. They do not see prison as a way of reforming criminals. They do not believe in the efficacy of education in changing standards of morality. When children talk about the school system they understand the purpose of being trained for employment and see the school as a social centre. They do not see it as a place to learn moral behaviour, even if teachers do. The sense that people should behave well to others because it is their moral duty to do so is replaced by the belief that if people did not behave well they would be punished. The pervading sense of society is that it is run through a sense of fear rather than guilt. This is the essential conservatism of these children. They do not see society in terms of social issues; how one creates the greatest good for the greatest number, or how one protects the weak from the strong. They are not taught to think about jurisprudence. Instead, the society they grow up in is presented to them in pragmatic terms. Their local systems of organization in and out of school are all run on a series of rules, to prevent people doing what they otherwise would. Just as schools are run on the mandate of authority, the personality of teachers and the imposition of rules, so children see society in similar terms.

The children who have access to the media, and to television in particular, are presented with a vision of society that is worldwide. They are made aware of the reality of war. They recognize the threat of nuclear weapons. So they know that the global context in which they live is a fearful one. Their classrooms might be havens of peace, and their only conflicts and fears the arguments with acquaintances or the threat of bullying. But they learn their

157

mathematics and read their books, at the same time knowing about death through starvation and conflict. Five- and 6-year-old children are concerned with the threat of nuclear war. They are even more fearful than older children who seem to become accustomed to the idea.[19] Children of 6 make coherent comments on war and peace, and by the age of 7 present well-defined views on tactics.[20] As they grow older so they dwell more on the human cost of war. The horror of the great idea, nuclear destruction, is gradually replaced by more intimate acquaintance with individual suffering.

Presented with such universal facts it is not surprising that children have a bleak view of society. The question is whether this is peculiar of our time or whether it was always thus. A look at children's literature of fifty years ago or more reveals a very different tone; one of optimism about progress, and confidence in human judgements. The world was one of adventure, for heroes well wadded in self-belief. The tone has changed so much that the literature of *Chums* or *Boy's Own Paper* appears to us almost ridiculous in its optimism and chauvinism. The present generations have no such easy confidence. They are reminded daily of human folly and human frailty.

A loss of confidence in society as a whole can be accompanied by a loss of self-esteem. Although children are taught that they must compete to do well, whether in school or in their careers, such teaching is not accompanied by a deeper sense of purpose. If the views of society are bleak, then children will not expect more from themselves. Naturally children deplore hooliganism and crime. They are annoyed by both. But they are neither shocked nor puzzled. Such actions might be 'silly' or heinous, but inevitable. Whilst they themselves would not do the same they feel they will always be surrounded by bad behaviour.

Children's views do not consist of unrelieved gloom. They are caught up in private pleasures as well as private griefs. They are as much entertained by all their favourite programmes on television as they are reminded of the news. They know about all the acts of kindness that people do for each other and they can share their pleasures at school. But their analysis of society is a bleak one. They are not so much cynical as pragmatic. This is how the world is presented to them, not deliberately but by accident. All the previously hidden aspects of human nature, like child abuse, are now publicly shared. Children grow up in a context of awareness of what disasters take place all over the world. Those events which take place far away might not have as much salience as something that happens in the neighbourhood, but they are part of the mosaic of society. Children have to accept that it is so and make sense of their own part in society as best they can.

The question is what education can do to help children construct a view of society that is well thought out, and which would help them understand it better. Their understanding of themselves, after all, depends on their understanding of other people. A bleak view of human nature is not going to bring out the best in their own. Some would question what difference education can make, against the power of the family. Indeed the children themselves assume that people cannot change. This itself is a worrying negation of the central importance of education. We know the difference schools can make, and recognize the importance of 'ethos', of shared beliefs. And yet the children are being allowed to develop a pessimistic view of society because it is an issue that is generally ignored in the curriculum.

When the nature of the curriculum is discussed in general terms, it it difficult to argue against all the different kinds of qualities it is supposed to contain, spiritual and moral as well as cultural.[21] The aims and objectives make a curriculum sound like the core of education, nurturing every need of the individual child. But when the curriculum is put into practice it is harder to see the underlying purpose which informs it. Some would argue that the traditional school curriculum provides all needs. The skills of communication are allied to the knowledge of history and geography and aesthetic values are catered for in music and art. Others would argue that their own subject, like technology or physical education, covers *all* the attributes of the curriculum. But the fact is that the traditional subjects that are 'delivered' by the National Curriculum remain subjects — a mixture of skills and knowledge. We rarely see an inner purpose to the curriculum, an underlying belief in the power of education.

The curriculum seems like a given entity. But it is rarely presented as having a relevance to children's understanding of themselves and their circumstances. Each pupil will grow up with political choice, and personal responsibilities. These, in turn, depend on sophisticated knowledge of their own cultures and other people's. This implies the need for a close analysis of society, the kind that is addressed in serious newspapers every day. Instead children are given no real analysis at all, but the equivalent of headlines in tabloid newspapers. And out of this they are assumed to make something coherent.

The fear of a curriculum which addresses social issues is a curious phenomenon, not thought out. The association of political education with propaganda for someone else's party suggests that the width of politics is not well understood. There are a number of moves which suggest that there is a willingness to go a little way towards deepening the curriculum, but not too far. The urge to educate for economic awareness is a good example. Whilst 'peace studies' or 'development education' are eschewed as being politically biased, economic awareness, of private industry in the main, is considered to be without any sense of indoctrination. Economic awareness would, indeed, have no biases at all, if it were taken to its logical conclusion. Knowing about the world of work and how society organizes itself is not just about the manufacture and the sales of goods. Indeed, knowing how money is made, taken by itself, can have unforeseen consequences. In one example presented on television, a school is praised for its enterprise in making and selling furniture, until it is discovered that it is dealing with stolen goods. But knowing the whole context in which money is made is quite a different matter.

Economic awareness, if it were pursued properly as an informing principle in the curriculum, would include the whole world of work, from trades unions to government, from foreign trade to taxation. It would have many political dimensions and raise serious questions about the choices people make. It would need to address issues that underlie the most essential political concepts in geography as well as economics. There is no doubting the children's capacity to understand. Indeed, they have no choice but to try to understand since they are, through their parents, friends and experience, confronted with the evidence of decisions every day.

Children think about central issues of debate, like war and peace or race.[22] But they think about them in an unstructured way. They experience many of the subjects that are considered dangerous in case they become 'indoctrinated', and are forced to make premature judgements. These judgements are like the suspicions that inform the voters in elections. In the absence of analysis, children continue to acquire knowledge.

The purpose of the curriculum cannot altogether be kept from the children. They will endeavour to bring their own interpretations to it. But the possibilities that we have with the curriculum, in developing a coherent sense of purpose, should not be ignored. Each human being wishes to understand his or her place in society, and be able to communicate that understanding. All the major questions that seem to be ignored could become central to the curriculum. The present curriculum might be an orchestra of the powers of the mind, but it seems badly out of tune.

What is missing from the curriculum is an underlying sense of purpose, a relevance to the lives of children. They submit to what is presented to them, but much of their thinking takes place elsewhere, outside the formalities of the classroom. The curriculum covers traditional approaches to knowledge and also, through topics, ways of connecting different aspects of knowledge. But it does not address the issues that children are concerned with.

The curriculum in schools tends to lack a conceptual framework. This is not just a shared understanding by teachers but a coherent set of concepts to be understood by children. They can accumulate pieces of knowledge without making sense of them. Even those things that they experience do not necessarily make sense. The human need to put newly acquired knowledge into a framework is such that the resulting structure can be very makeshift or imbalanced. To take one example: children are usually aware of the countryside, with its animals and trees, its space and its farms. They eat the products of the countryside. And yet even those who live there do not organize their understanding of the underlying concept of the different kinds of farming, the needs being provided or the choices made.[23] The visual experience is separate from the conceptual understanding.

The children who spoke so freely about their views of society have presented their views with consistency and clarity. They did not dwell on what they thought of school, of what they had not learned at school. But their views should give us pause for thought about what we do in school, and what we expect from school.

There was a time, perhaps, when all had a framework of beliefs.

There are places, certainly, where beliefs are rigidly imposed. But we are accustomed to the notion of questioning, even if not used to answers. The children show that they have acquired a series of messages and symbols about the society in which they live. They are not optimistic about the future. They accept the need for powerful forces to support law and order. And yet they have no strong belief in the incorruptibility of such power. They despise people who riot and they deplore football hooligans, but see no solutions except more control. But they do not believe in those who are in control, as if they too contributed to the circumstances that create riots. They accept the power of politicians but also their persuadability by those close to them; they argue for the rights of demonstration and yet are cynical about individual justice; they believe in the power of the law but not its efficacy; they assume the rights of all to have jobs but despise those who cannot get them. In all, they argue for the need for powerful controls, but they do not seek justification for such control beyond pragmatic necessity.

Children are acquiring underlying beliefs which form their behaviour as well as their views. There are bound to be connections between their fundamental attitudes and the way they approach their work in schools. Their belief in sanctions, in fear and control, rather than belief and reason, suggests several things which have a bearing on the society of the future. It implies an acceptance of the way things are which is neither optimistic, nor militant. And it implies a belief in controls and punishment in society which responds to the characteristics of individual human nature.

When the interviews that form the evidence of the book were carried out, the intention was to find out the extent of children's knowledge. What emerged shows not only the acute awareness of children but a consistently shared attitude. It needs to be taken into account by all who care about the future.

NOTES AND REFERENCES

1. Rutter, M., Maughan, B., Mortimore, P., and Ouston, J. *Fifteen Thousand Hours — Secondary Schools and Their Effects on Children.* London: Open Books, 1979; Mortimore, P., Sammons, P., Stoll, L., Lewis, D., and Ecob, R. *School Matters: The Junior Years.* London: Open Books, 1988.
2. Ashcroft, K. 'The teacher and the ethos of the school.' In C. Cullingford, *The Primary Teacher.* London: Cassell, 1989, pp. 75–94.

3. Between *Konkorrenz* and *Wettbewerb*.
4. Cullingford, C. *The Inner World of the School*. London: Cassell, 1991.
5. Katz, E., and Lazarsfeld, P.F. *Personal Influence: The Part Played by People in the Flow of Mass Communications*. Glencoe, IL: Free Press, 1955.
6. Bowles, S., and Gintis, H. *Schooling in Capitalist America*. London: Routledge & Kegan Paul, 1976.
7. Pollard, A. *The Social World of the Primary School*. London: Holt, Rinehart & Winston, 1985.
8. Kapferer, J.-N. *Rumeurs: Le plus vieux média du monde*. Paris: Editions du Seuil, 1987.
9. Newcomb, T.M. 'An approach to the study of communication acts.' *Psychological Review* **60**, 393–404, 1953.
10. Dunn, J. *The Beginnings of Social Understanding*. Oxford: Basil Blackwell, 1988.
11. Dunn, J., *op. cit.*, p. 65.
12. Bauer, R. 'Limits of persuasion.' *Harvard Business Review* **36**(5), 105–110, 1958.
13. Belson, J.W.A. *The Impact of Television: Methods and Findings in Programme Research*. London: Crosby Lockwood, 1967.
14. Cullingford, C. *Children and Television*. Aldershot: Gower, 1984, Chapter 6, pp. 49–59.
15. Elias, N. *The Civilising Process*: Vol. 1, 1978; Vol. 2, 1982. Oxford: Basil Blackwell.
16. Egan, K. *Education and Psychology: Plato, Piaget and Scientific Psychology*. New York: Teachers College Press, 1983.
17. Schrank, J. (ed.) *Understanding Mass Media*. Skokie, IL: National Textbook Library, 1975.
18. DES, *Discipline in Schools*. Report on the Committee of Enquiry chaired by Lord Elton. London: HMSO, 1989.
19. Tizard, B. 'Impact of the nuclear threat on children's development.' In M. Richards and P. Light (eds), *Children of Social Worlds*. London: Polity Press, 1986.
20. Cooper, P. 'The development of the concept of war.' *Journal of Peace Research* **1**(1), 1–17, 1965.
21. DES, *The Curriculum from 5 to 16. Curriculum Matters 2*. London: HMSO, 1985.
22. Finn, G. 'Children and controversial issues: Some myths and misinterpretations identified and challenged from a cognitive developmental perspective.' *Cambridge Journal of Education* **20**(1), 5–27, 1990.
22. Harrison, L. 'The junior school child's understanding of farming.' Unpublished M. Phil thesis, Brighton Polytechnic, 1990.

Name Index

Subject Index